Tupela Go Wokabout
by Gerri Parsons, 2003

© Copyright 2004, Gerri Parsons.
All rights reserved.

No part of this publication may be reproduced, stored in a retrieval system, or transmitted, in any form or by any means, electronic, mechanical, photocopying, recording, or otherwise, without the written prior permission of the author.

Note for Librarians: a cataloguing record for this book that includes Dewey Decimal Classification and US Library of Congress numbers is available from the National Library of Canada. The complete cataloguing record can be obtained from the National Library's online database at:
www.nlc-bnc.ca/amicus/index-e.html
ISBN 1-4120-4031-0
Printed in Victoria, BC, Canada

TRAFFORD

Offices in Canada, USA, Ireland, UK and Spain

This book was published *on-demand* in cooperation with Trafford Publishing. On-demand publishing is a unique process and service of making a book available for retail sale to the public taking advantage of on-demand manufacturing and Internet marketing. On-demand publishing includes promotions, retail sales, manufacturing, order fulfilment, accounting and collecting royalties on behalf of the author.

Book sales in Europe:
Trafford Publishing (UK) Ltd., Enterprise House, Wistaston Road Business Centre, Wistaston Road, Crewe CW2 7RP UNITED KINGDOM
phone 01270 251 396 (local rate 0845 230 9601)
facsimile 01270 254 983; info.uk@trafford.com

Book sales for North America and international:
Trafford Publishing, 6E–2333 Government St.,
Victoria, BC V8T 4P4 CANADA
phone 250 383 6864 (toll-free 1 888 232 4444)
fax 250 383 6804; email to bookstore@trafford.com

www.trafford.com/robots/04-1838.html

10 9 8 7 6 5 4 3 2 1

DONATION. 10.04.

Contents

Forward	7
A Trip Across Canada by Train - 2002	9
1977 and Cuba	32
A Visit to Haiti - 1987	50
Two Tickets On the E&N - 1990	56
A Trip Down Under - 1990	58
50-year School Reunion - 1994	65
B.C. Rail Cariboo Prospector - 1998	72
The Royal Hudson - 1991	74
China	76
Princess Auto Inventor's Fair - 2000	90

FOREWORD

Charlie and I have made many trips around B.C., with our sawmill and/or children's workshop, to schools and fairs, many trips for conferences and meetings, trips for medical reasons and, of course, trips to visit our family and friends. These, I will not mention in this book. Our 2½ years in PNG has been described in detail in my previous book, *Sawdust In My Gotches*. I will not repeat it here. However, I will repeat our trip to Cuba and write about some of the other trips that we have made that were not business trips or family trips, like our trips to Haiti, Australia and New Zealand, our trip across Canada on VIA Rail and to Victoria on E & N Railroad, as well as other train trips, like B.C. Rail and the Royal Hudson.

A Trip Across Canada By Train

It was a trip Charlie and I had thought about for some time. As was my habit, I always stop at the travel agent in the mall, just to see the pamphlets and notices. One day, I noticed a pamphlet on trips by train. In it was an advertisement about a 30-days Rail Pass across Canada for a reasonable price each.

The agent was not too busy at the time, so I inquired about the trip. After getting all the details, I said to Charlie, "Let's take the train across Canada." This was in May 2002.

Charlie and I went into the agency a week later to make arrangements for our trip, in October, to celebrate Charlie's 80th and my 77th birthdays. As the price changed on the 15th of October, we had to wait for a few days later. Our birthdays were on the 12th and 13th of October. After phoning the VIA Rail office, the agent found out that the train was filled up until the 20th, so she suggested we book our passage as soon as we could. We decided to go on the 20th of October. We ordered our tickets and set the schedule of our travel. We planned to travel from Vancouver, straight through to Halifax, visit our former Field Staff Officer in Hammins Plains, then visit a friend in New Brunswick. The friend lived in Mirramichi, which is on the train route, so we could take the train back from there. We could travel as far as Toronto, where we could get another train down to the States to see my sister-in-law, who lived just outside of Buffalo in Middleport, New York, then take the train back to Toronto and on home again. Those were our plans.

We picked up our tickets, got our travel insurance and bought a new travel bag for Charlie ten days before we were to leave. Pack, unpack, pack again, discard this or that, unpack again, decide if we needed this or did not need that, repack again and take our chances that we did the right thing. On Saturday, October 20th, at 7:30 a.m., we took a taxi to the bus station, where we were to catch the bus for Vancouver. Being diabetic, I had had a bite to eat and, of course, had my tea in bed. Who knew when I would get tea in bed again. It was raining, that morning, but this did not bother us, as we were at the start of another new adventure.

Although the bus was a big one, it manoeuvred the winding coast road very well. It was sad to see the clear-cuts, but was good to know the trees will grow again. Trees are not like gas and oil, which, when gone, are gone for a another million years. Forests are the only renewable resource we have.

We were surprised at the little choice we had for breakfast on the first ferry. I slept most of the way from Earl's Cove to Gibsons. There were lots of sailboats off Gibsons. It looked like there might have been a race or something.

As we went over Lions Gate Bridge, I noticed lots of people out for their daily stroll along the seawalk. Going through Stanley Park must be a pleasant interlude from the hustle and bustle of the city for some people. As I looked at the glass buildings, it made me wonder what would happen if we had an earthquake. It was nice to see that the old buildings, like the Burrard and Sun Buildings, were still there.

Vancouver bus-train station, the first leg of our trip over. During a three-hour wait at the station, we had some supper, walked around and snooped in all the small shops. There were not too many waiting for the VIA Rail train, but there were between 75 and 100 waiting for the Amtrack train to Seattle. We were in the coach, but the conductor gave us nice soft pillows and blankets to sleep with. The seats were comfortable, even though they were a little bit short for some people to stretch out on. It was good, if you were in a 4-seat place, as you could stretch out across the seats. I had no problem stretching out on one seat, as I could pull my legs up and fit nicely on the seat. Charlie and I ate all our meals on the train. People said they were expensive, but we found that they were not more expensive, and is some cases less, than in some of our local restaurants. As the meals were big, Charlie and I used to share one meal. The meals were very good, so they were worth every penny spent. Although it was dark out, you could see a lot because of the full moon shining. Maybe it was the Thompson, or maybe the Fraser River, but there were whitecaps on it as we passed. There were only a few places I recognized, even though I had been through the area many times by car. It all looks so different from the train, especially at night. When we went through the Ashcroft area, it looked like snow, but could have been sage brush. It could have been granite rock.

The one thing about train travel is that you can get up and walk around, even if it is only in the aisle.

North Kamloops was our first long stop (40 minutes). There was not much to see at this station, as it was not much more than a train yard with just one small building. We got off for a walk, but it was chilly, so we did not go far before we got back on the train. Some men, who just had to have their smokes, got off the train and braved the cold. The toilets are locked when the train is in the station, which proved an inconvenience for some people who forgot to go before we came into the station and, also, because there was no place to go in the station house, which was locked. The train took on water and other necessities.

Another day is dawning, after a good night's sleep. We are nearing Valemont and the Rockies are in view now, above the timber that the train goes through. We must have gone higher during the night, as we are now above a deep valley. This area, like many others, is truly beautiful. That is why it is called 'Beautiful B.C.' As the kids say, "It is awesome." The yellow of the alders and maples can be seen through the green of the cedars and pines. Here and there is a stately, but bare, birch. Sticking above the other trees are old, dead snags that show evidence of a past fire. Other snags can be seen with their tops broken off. All along the train track are telephone poles, and the occasional freight train passes us.

One thing I forgot to mention earlier was the painting on the cement enbutments of the bridges, or Skytrain, and the cement walls we passed as we travelled out of New Westminster. Here was the work of some unknown artists. Some were a bit weird, but many were well done. Here was talent wasted, but a pleasure to see by those travelling. In several different train yards, or on a train passing, we noticed some good painting on the box cars and tank cars.

At this point, I would like to tell you about the train. It was a long train with two engines (three for travelling through the mountains), three baggage cars, three or four coaches, three dome cars with diners and/or lounges, two separate diners, six-or-more sleepers or compartments. The above is only an estimate, as I did not count them. On the frieght trains that passed there were from 60 to 130 cars, not including the engines.

In the coach, where we were, there were two toilets. This proved a great convenience for me. The train was kept immaculately clean and the attendants were there all the time to address any concern we might have. Every comfort was provided, whether you were economy class in the coaches or first class in the sleepers. This made the trip very pleasant.

As we passed high above the highway, in the mountains, there were a few clouds around, but it was still a good day. As we came down to the lower level, we passed some very old farms. Snow was beginning to appear on the mountain tops. Here and there, we would see old deserted cabins, houses and barns. We are now passing a small town where the people have not come awake yet. The businesses still display their 'closed' signs. The sign on the track says 'Valemount.' One sign on a hotel, 'Log & Rail Bar,' which I found very different. It was kinda neat, so I thought at the time.

Change your time from Pacific Time to Mountain Time. Out of the large window in the diner, we noticed the beautiful view of Moose Lake and the surrounding area as we ate our meal. There was a very nice young couple who were eating with us. He was a bull rider in the rodeos. The attendant at the diner would always seat someone with you for every meal. It was not always the same person. He tried to match couples with couples and single people together.

We had a one-hour stop in Jasper, so Charlie and I went for a long walk around the town. Jasper is a quaint little place. All the notices, etc. are in both English and French. We noticed this was true in most places across Canada.

Thank goodness for the modern technology or communication between the trains. The approaching train knows we are coming and our engineer is aware of the approaching freight train, so he has time to move into a siding to let it pass. It is amazing how synchronized the trains are. It was nice to watch, from the dome car, the lights along the track that told the engineer if the track was clear. The light would be green, but when the engine had passed, it would turn red. From the dome, you can see where you are going and can see farther away. When we were in the area of Hinton-Edson, Alberta, there were lots of old telephone poles with no wires. They still had the glass insulators on them, which could mean a lot of money to some collectors, but it is nice to leave them where they are for the sake of heritage.

Breakfast is always the same, between 6:30 and 9:00, with lunch from 12:00 to 2:30. Supper depends on the stop where we are, but is usually 5:00 and 8:00 p.m. As we are a little bit late, we are just whizzing along tonight.

We have not seen much wild life, except the dead deer we saw beside the road near Stillwater, in the Powell River area. At one spot, coming out of Vancouver, we saw about 100 black crows, all flying together. We did see some gulls around Jasper, and large black crows here and there as we went along. A couple of times, we saw a large bird on a snag, which could have been an eagle or raven.

We did notice lots of old cars and other machinery in people's back yards. There were not as many cows as we had expected. Perhaps this was because the farmers did not have enough feed and had to sell their stock. There seemed to be more horses than there were cattle. However, there were lots of round bales of hay on the ground, but not as much as usual.

The Big City of Edmonton:
There is development all along the way from Spruce Grove to Edmonton. We got off the train and went into the station, where we found a large number of passengers waiting to board the train, so we went back onto the train and waited for it to move again, so we could go to supper. We were again joined by the same young couple.

We made a stop in Biggar, Saskatchewan. If we stopped before this, I was unaware, as I was asleep most of the time.

There was quite a nip in the air, but we got out of the train anyway, for a walk in Saskatoon. Like many places where we stopped, the station was on the outskirts of town, in the railroad yard.

After a good sleep, a breakfast at Rivers, Sask. and a wait for a freight train, we are on our way again, with a brief stop in Portage la Prairie for people to get on and others to leave. The sounds of the train wheels again put me to sleep. When we got off in Winnipeg, we had to go into the station for safety reasons. Winnipeg station is a big station, like the one in Vancouver. We knew our way around this station, as we had been here before, when we went to the Princess Auto's Inventors Fair. That time, we had a whole day at the station.

This time, we only had time to go to the rest room. The first time, we went to a big mall, the museum and the parks near the station. There is a lot to do around the station. We planned to have lunch in or near the station, but the train was an hour late, so we had lunch on the train. The train travelled slower through a few small towns and along some small lakes with ice on them. It was getting cold in the area of Ontario. The scenery had changed from the flat, wide country of the prairies to rocks and trees. The trees are small in diameter, but very tall. We were beginning to see the odd larger one, and the hills were getting taller. It was somewhat like the interior of B.C. There were lots of beautiful lakes.

Stop at Sioux, get off the train for some air, take two steps from the train, slip on the ice and fall on my bum. I twisted my knee, but not seriously. I got back on the train before I could fall again. The train started to go faster so that we could make up some time. A big moon was shining, lighting up the trees, which were covered with snow, making them gleam through the dark night.

Here we are. It is our fourth day of travel. The train is moving right along. We have passed many places not mentioned, as the train went by too fast. There were no signs to state what they were, or I did not notice the signs. As we passed a winding river, just past Sudbury, it made me think how nice it would be to be cruising along in a houseboat. I have had the same feeling at some other lakes we passed.

Toronto Station: It was a long walk to the main station, where we had supper, then made the long walk back to the train, which was a new train. There were advertisements in the station, telling of all the wonderful features of the train. It was not so wonderful. The seats were too close. It was more modern, but certainly not as comfortable. It had a table for your cup, or whatever it was, if you knew the secret to set it up. There was no place for small luggage, like on the older trains. Only a small thin place above that was a square. It was meant for a briefcase, I think. It was bought from a company in England and was meant for an inter-suburban train (a train that commutes between two cities or suburbs).

    The new train is much brighter and shiny-new, but we do not like it. The seats are about a foot above an aisle that runs the length of the car. We noticed a couple of passengers fall when they tried either to get into the seat or get down out of it. Thank goodness it was only for one night. The bathrooms were small and inconvenient. As we waited for the train to start, we noticed some double-decker trains that were part of the subway that goes under the city.

    We had to get up early to disembark at Montreal. The station at Montreal is a much bigger station than either Vancouver or Winnipeg. In fact, it was bigger than any station we have been in, including plane terminals (except Honolulu). There must have been fifty-or-more food places, five or six bars, five or six beauty salons, many small stores, like tobacco shops, grocery stores, a couple of pharmacies, banks, etc., VIA Rail offices and other offices, like Human Resources. We wandered around the station. As there was so much to see, we are not sure we saw it all. However, we did fill in the 10 hours we had there. We went outside for a walk around the building after lunch. Back in the station, rest and wait for the departure of the train. We found some old newspapers, which we read. One thing that was better than the smaller stations was that there were more than one women's toilets. There were no lineups here. In some places, there were long lineups for one or two toilets. On the train, the toilets are closed when it is in a station. They close them five minutes before you arrive in a large station like this one. The reason for this is because the train did not have a holding tank, so they did not want a discharge in the station. Montreal was like Toronto, with its huge buildings. Some looked to be at least 50 stories high. Not for the world would I like to live in one of those high apartment buildings, or work in one of those tall buildings either. It would be too scary.

    It had been a long wait in the station at Montreal, so we had lots of teas. On the train again. We were amazed at the development from just before Toronto to well into New Brunswick. The houses we saw in Ontario and in the Maritimes were much different than those in B.C. They have peaked roofs, with gabled windows. They are mostly wood frame or brick. We have been going along beside the highway a lot, as we could see lots of cars, which got less in the evening. There were lots of big trucks, some with lights like a Christmas tree.

There is the ocean. We have gone from the Pacific Ocean to the Atlantic. Oh, Oh. That is not a nice sight to see when you are travelling on a train. There were twisted freight cars lying in the ditch along side of the track. They must have been carrying oil or grain, as there were a couple of oil or grain cars amongst the wreck. There were about five or six cars. They looked like they had been there for a while. There was a crew working there that looked like they were cleaning the debris up. There were a couple of bulldozers on the site. It was a good idea to clean up the mess, as it could put some people off train travel.

The train whistles, not only at the crossings, but also before it approaches a stop at a station. This is to warn people that the train is coming into the station so that, if there are people waiting, they will be prepared to board or greet someone that may be getting off. A bar comes down at most crossings, but at others there are only the lights. A bar is at all the main crossings and there are flashing lights at all crossings. The train also goes slowly before it approaches a town. The clickety-clack of the train wheels bothered Charlie, but put me to sleep. Like in other things, I am always the opposite.

We are now at Turo, N.S., which means we are nearly finished the first half of our travels. Some strange or interesting things we have seen:- Black, shiny dirt on the side of the river in New Brunswick; a wooden cow and cart with pumpkins in it on the front lawn of a house just before Halifax; hundreds of ducks on a pond outside a village in N.B.; lots of lakes, rivers and other water bodies; different equipment in a school yard in Montreal, such as a group of poles with string strung every which-way between them and a game painted in the cement that I had never seen before. The equipment looked like it would require more strength than that in our school yards. In Montreal, and after, it would have been nice to be able to speak French, as most people on the train spoke French and there was some difficulty, at times, communicating with some of the other passengers. The staff on the train, of course, spoke both English and French. The only wildlife we saw were ducks in Maple Ridge and crows in N.B. Many people were disappointed. One couple did see a moose and a couple of goats. Of course, we did see lots of cows and horses in the fields on the prairies, lower B.C. and Nova Scotia.

Chris Bryant, our former field staff officer when we were in P.N.G. [Papua New Guinea], met us at the train station in Halifax. We all went to his office, so he could check up on his messages. Then we went out to his house, where his wife Syble had a lovely supper prepared. We sat around till about 10 p.m., visiting. Then we were off to bed, where I fell asleep as soon as my head hit the pillows. The next morning, after breakfast, we went outside, where Charlie cut down some dead trees for Chris. Later, we went to the home of a relative of Chris's, where we had a pumpkin-carving party. Charlie carved a pumpkin like our prime minister, which lots of people thought was funny. After lots of goodies and our pumpkin carving, we left again. Each person took his/her pumpkin home for Hallowe'en. Charlie left his there, with our host. They gave prizes for the different pumpkins. Everyone got something. Charlie and I got a Cape Breton Lighthouse candle. It was a memory of our trip.

Chris then took us to Peggy's Cove, which sure was windy and cold. We walked around a bit by the lighthouse, which was closed for the season. Then we went into the restaurant for a hot cup of tea. I phoned Krista from there. I had meant to call her with my calling card, but I pushed the wrong button on the phone and the call was collect. Krista did not mind, as she was anxious for us to call. We then purchased some post cards, but not as many as I wanted; neither did we take any photos, as I would have liked, but the weather was poor for photo taking. Chris drove us on another route back to his house, so we could see another part of the area. Over the years, I have seen many pictures of Nova Scotia that seem to always picture Peggy's Cove and, when you read about Nova Scotia, it always mentions that place, as it seems to be the emblem of the province. Now I can say I have been there. It is just like the pictures, a quiet little village with white houses on the edge of the sea. It was very windy and I almost got blown away. Chris joked and said, "There goes Gerri, flying over that cliff to the east."

It was a wonderful day, Chris and Syble were marvellous hosts. We had such a good time with them.

On Sunday, October 27, we packed our gear again to start on our first leg home. Syble made us some delicious turkey sandwiches to eat on the train. Last night, Chris and I watched the movie *Hard Run*. It was about an armored-car driver who got burglarized by some bandits, but he escaped with the money. The bandits pursued him, a corrupt sherrif got involved and there was a lot of violence. Of course, there was a girl involved and a bit of romance brewing. Charlie had gone to bed and Syble fell asleep on the couch.

It was so nice to talk about old times in P.N.G., as we all had many memories. It had been a wonderful visit.

There was a change in the time, from daylight saving to standard time. It was a good thing Chris phoned to check the schedule, as he discovered the train left a half-hour earlier than my schedule said. We noticed, on our way to the train station, the new high-rise buildings that stood among the older buildings of brick and stone. Halifax is an old city. We also noticed the ships in the harbor, but not too many. Chris had shown us a couple of places when we first came, but we did not really see Halifax, as we were only there a couple of nights. We plan to be at Rodger's longer.

Here we are at the train station. It was smaller than any of the bigger stations we were in, like Montreal and Vancouver. There were no cafes or stores. It must have rained the night before we arrived, as there was water all around, with one big puddle at the train station.

Chris and Charlie took photos and, as we waited, we had time to do some more talking.

We are on our way again. There are lots of apartment buildings beside the tracks; some are very old. I am not sure I would like to live in any of them. As we pass the harbor, we notice grain elevators, oil tankers, and buildings associated with freight. Freight travel is either by boat or by train. There are lots of rocks along the way, with the usual paintings and writings on them, as well as on the cement posts.

The leaves in the east are more beautiful than those we see in the west. They are different, with bright reds, yellows, tans and blues. These are often mixed in with the greens. The trees are smaller and of a different variety. They look more like bushes than trees. The houses and buildings we saw were old and quaint. Some of the rocks we saw were cracked. I'm not sure if this was natural or the result of blasting when they were building the railroad. Most of the trains that passed us were very long. One had 110 cars, some of which were double-container height. It was raining and we noticed the sea was very rough. I am glad I am on a train and not on a boat or plane. Looking at the houses, so close to the track, makes me wonder what it would be like to live in one of them. I imagine it would be very noisy, but, then, maybe the people get used to the noise. There is so much to write about, looking out the train window. There is so much scenery, but it is hard to write it all down–quaint little churches, a police car racing down the road, beautiful expansive lakes, rivers and canals. There are some high hills, but no mountains–or what we know as mountains. We noticed several areas of flooding on some of the farms and in the ditches. Also, the rivers and lakes seemed higher. In one place there were about six cows on an island in a small river or stream, or perhaps it was a field before. We saw more cows on our way back west than we saw coming east. Perhaps the timing was different. On Sunday, there was a lot of equipment in the yards, idle. Seeing the bales of hay lying in the open fields made me wonder how they survive the cold winters. The train was going too fast for me to recognize the signs on the side of the track, so I was not sure where we were. It was too dark to see much of the landscape, anyway.

Roger, a CUSO who was with us in P.N.G., was at the station in Miramachi. We then went to his house, which was a small place in Newcastle, a suburb of Miramachi. We sat up late, drinking tea and talking. Roger had a big picture album of his time in P.N.G., which we all enjoyed going over, remembering our good times. On Monday, Roger took us for an enjoyable ride around the area. Then we went back to his house for an enjoyable dinner. We had stopped twice for snacks at Tim Horton's. That place turned out to be Roger's favorite place, like Robin's is ours here in Powell River and other places. Roger had taken us for a drive to the beach to see the Top of Island of Lie Miscore and the Tip of New Brunswick. Quebec was on the left and New Foundland on the right, across the sea. The smell of the ocean was wonderful. We walked along the beach, took pictures and viewed the lighthouse. Roger then took us to see some falls, which were more like rapids. It was getting dark, so, instead of taking a back road that he wanted to show us, Roger took us back the way we had come, by Bathurst Road and Highway #8. It had been another enjoyable and interesting day. We were learning more about Canada every day. Roger's deceased wife had many books, including ones by my favorite author, Agatha Christy. I selected one with her short stories and started reading it.

Tuesday was a wonderful day that started with a brisk walk around a couple of blocks near Roger's house. After breakfast, Roger took us for another ride. We went to lunch at Tim Horton's, then to a park outside Miramachi, where we went on a boardwalk, out to the sand dunes. This was another great adventure for us. The wind was strong, but not too cold. On the way home, we stopped at a peat moss manufacturing place. We then went to Chatham, where Charlie and I stayed at Roger's mother's house while he went to the doctor. His mother was not home, so Charlie read the paper while I watched TV. We both had tea. It was back to Roger's to change our clothes for dinner at a Chinese restaurant. Then we picked Roger's mother up and we all went to an enjoyable concert, where we listened to the singing of the Irishman, John McDunmetle. Also featured, was a group of two young girls and two young boys. One of the girls, who was only about 11 or twelve, was very talented with the fiddle and dancing a jig. She was one of the best fiddlers I have ever heard. Her fellow performers were very good dancers, too. After the concert, Roger, his mother, Charlie and I went to have coffee–at Tim Horton's, of course. Roger gassed up, as he discovered his gas was low.

Today, we also went to see the Fishermen's Memorial, where 36 fishermen died several years ago when their boats were caught in a violent storm. When the boats left the harbor, the sea was dead calm, but, during the afternoon, a violent wind came up with no warning. As the boats neared the harbor, they were overturned and the men in them were drowned. All along the coast were pieces of the boats and many of the bodies. Those boats that stayed out at sea and weathered the storm somehow survived. It was the boats that attempted to get back into port that were destroyed.

Wednesday: We were up early, went for a walk up one street, then over a side street (which came to a dead end). Go through a field, along an old road, which came out on a street which, lo and behold, was only two blocks from Roger's. Charlie said, "It is not that way; it is over that hill." So, off we tramped, about six more blocks, then decided we had better head the other way. We noticed some men working on the road and we went up that road, only to discover another dead end. We retraced our steps to a road where I recognized the school at the end of it and knew it was the school near Roger's. We followed that road and were back at his place. Roger had breakfast waiting for us.

Later, we went with Roger to see a monastery, a convent and a monument park for the Ascension of the Virgin Mary to Heaven. This is a belief of the Catholics that Mary was delivered to heaven by the angels. Other churches do not believe this.

We stopped in a small convenience store, where we all got a drink. I had hot chocolate, but Roger and Charlie had coffee. We then went down the road to another falls. We continued down a trail back to the parking lot along a beautiful stream that meandered through the woods. At one place, there was a covered bridge, known by the locals as "the Kissing Bridge." Of course, Charlie and I had a kiss. As it was again getting late and Roger was not sure of the roads in that district, we retraced out steps back to Miramachi, where Roger again cooked a wonderful supper. He had put it in the slow cooker before we left. His friend, Allen, joined us for the meal that night.

Roger had a little grey, lovable dog named Fritz, who was about seven years old. He just loved attention, but was not house broken, which, sometimes, was a problem that I am sure I could not tolerate long. My dogs were trained before they were a year old.

When we were at a store, where Roger gassed up, I bought a scratch-and-win and won two dollars.

Another place we went to today, was the prison where Roger works. We could only view it from the outside. Boy, what a fence around the grounds. There was wire with barbs (about six strands of sharp stuff) at the top. Roger said it was an electric fence, too. So I don't think anyone would try to go over the fence.

Friday: Our last day at Roger's and the second leg of our journey back home. It was Hallowe'en. We went to the school to see their workshops, but it was not convenient at the time. Charlie did, however, have a long conversation with the teacher. I went to the library to inquire if they would be interested in my book. The librarian asked to see the book. Later, after some discussion, we decided to give the school library a copy of the book. When we went out that afternoon, I took a copy to the school. We then went to the store, where I cashed in my scratch-and-win bingo card. When speaking to Krista by phone, earlier, I learned that one of her friends lived just outside of Miramachi. So Roger took us out to their farm. We had met Cindy, Krista's friend, before, when we visited Krista in Dawson

Creek. We remembered Cindy and she remembered us. She was so happy we had come to see them. We had a most enjoyable visit, but did not see much of the farm, as Cindy had to go out someplace. After our visit, Roger took us to lunch. We picked up the dog Fritz, then went to Friendly Fort Cove Park for a walk around the lake, or cove. At Harbour Park, we walked around, viewing the monuments and a replica of a sailing ship. We also went to a small park in Miramachi to see the place where Lord Beaverbrook was buried. Then back to Roger's for dinner. Allen and another friend were there. We all had another wonderful meal cooked by Roger. As it was Hallowe'en, Roger had lots of goodies for the children, and every once-in-a-while, the doorbell would be rung by the trick-or-treaters. Roger took us to the train station while Allen and his friend gave out the goodies. After a short wait, we were on the next step home again. Except for the lighted areas, there is not much to see at night.

    Our first stop, Rimonski, must have been a very religious town, as there were many crosses, some of which were also crucifixes. There were a lot of people around, even though it was past midnight. At the station, there were a group of young people who ran along beside the train, shouting something, but I could not tell what they were saying. They may have been seeing some friends off, or perhaps they were teammates leaving town. We must have been going beside a highway, because there were big trucks going by. There was a three-bunk logging truck travelling along at the same speed as the train. It made me think of our son Marty and wonder if he was travelling along some road up north in B.C. at that time, too. There seemed to be quite a few young boys on the train. Perhaps they were the ones that group of youths at the station were yelling at. Most of the people on the train were asleep, but, after I had a nap, I found it hard to get back to sleep. Another thing I noticed in Rimonski was the many apartment houses along the side of the tracks.

    In Campbellton, we noticed a lot of heavy industry that looked like oil or gas installations. One thing I noticed in Nova Scotia, Quebec and Ontario was the number of old churches, many that were of large grey brick or stone. In some places, the tallest or largest places around were the churches. In other places, the churches were smaller and made of wood. As I mentioned before, the lights seemed to be continuous from shortly after we entered Quebec, to all the way to Montreal and beyond.

There is much to wonder about, like: What is in those big tanks? What kind of industry is going on in those big buildings? Is that building a school, an institution, a hospital or, perhaps a prison? How many people live in that big house? Somehow, the houses in the area of the Maritimes seem more homey than in other places. Canada must have grown a lot in the last 50 years, because I was taught, in school [in Buffalo, New York], that it was mostly ice and snow, with very little development. Of course, I knew better, as many of my relatives lived in Canada. I am so happy that we made this trip and got to see parts of our great country that we had never seen before. We saw some of the old parts of Canada and learned some of its history. It has been a great adventure, seeing all the old buildings of the original Canada and the homes of the original dwellers.

There seems to be a lot more smoke, or steam, coming from the plants. Perhaps that is because it was on the week-end when we came through before. If I had learned French, I would know what place we are passing through. Whatever it is, it is large. There are lots of lights, buildings, tanks and steam. The city here is Rivier Du Lorup. There are signs all around, but they are all in French. I wish I had a better knowledge of words so that I could describe the things I see and do it in a more dramatic way. I have done and seen some great things, but I cannot describe them the way I see or feel them. For instance; although I do not like the city, I get a thrill out of seeing the lights of a city at night, especially if we are above it. I could say the lights are like diamonds in the night, but that would not really describe the beauty of them. I wish I could describe the charm I see in some of the old houses and buildings and the thrill I get at seeing them.

As we get nearer Montreal, it seems it is just one continuous city for miles and miles, even thouogh we still have four hours to go to get to reach the station. I am not sure where we are now, but it is snowing. We are moving backwards and there is a couple of inches of snow on the ground.

Ah, Montreal! Another day, another leg of our journey. As in Vancouver, the cars are now bumper to bumper, as people rush on their way into the city, probably to go to work. Good thing I phoned Elsie, my sister-in-law, as she thought we were coming tomorrow instead of today. Thank Goodness the train to Toronto is not the same one we had coming from Toronto to Montreal. This trip from Montreal to Toronto will be much more pleasant, as it will be in daylight.

Brockville, the place where my dad was born and where Grandpa Cooke was raised.

Kingston, where I have many memories, both good and bad. The home of my grandparents, where my mother was raised. The place where I spent many enjoyable vacations.

As we get into Ontario, we begin to see deserted farm houses and land. Here is Toronto, with its high buildings and rushing traffic. There was a bit of confusion in the station, but we got it all straightened out. Have a bit to eat and wait, and wait, and wait. There is a mad rush to board the train, but, as we are seniors, we can pre-board. What a mad-house the departure area is. Lineups are sometimes 30-to-50 people long, sometimes more. Our train is almost filled to capacity. It was interesting to watch the large number of people rushing to catch what I assumed was the subway, and the same large number coming from the subway. Some of the people probably are commuters who do the same thing twice every day. Since it is Friday, people are most likely going home, or some place, for the weekend. As the train goes along, it is city all the way. There is no break in the lights. As there are many junctions and crossings between Toronto and Niagara Falls, the train is constantly blowing its whistle.

Niagara Falls, Ontario, what a city! All lights, with casinos, night clubs, haunted houses–every kind of tourist trap you can think of. Seeing the revolving restaurant reminds me of our trip with Benita in 1978.

Glen and Elsie (my sister-in-law and her son) were there at the Niagara Falls station to meet us. They took us to dinner. Then we drove across the border to Elsie's house. We had no trouble crossing the border. The customs official just asked each of us where we were born. At Elsie's, we settled in, then had pie and tea. It was very late when we turned into bed.

After a good breakfast, Charlie and I went for a walk down into the village area, where we went into a café for coffee. As Charlie had only Canadian money, and the waitress was unsure of the exchange, it cost us $4.78 for two cups of coffee. Charlie had given the girl $5 and got 82 cents change in American coins, so it was probably a few cents less in Canadian. This was a day for relaxing, reminiscing and enjoying our visit with Elsie. Later, we went for another walk, where we met a few of Elsie's neighbors. Elsie and I talked until late again.

On Sunday, we took another walk after breakfast, watched TV (a good movie with Judy Garland) and then got dressed for dinner with my nephew. Elsie took us to a Classic restaurant, where Glen had made reservations. We were an hour early, so we ordered coffee and sat at the table to wait. Larry, my nephew, and his wife came in and were walking around when I went up to them and asked them to join us. Larry said, "Oh, I'm waiting for my brother."

So I said, "Why don't you join your mother?"

Larry was surprised. "You are Aunt Gerri," he said, as he hugged me.

Larry joined us and Glen came shortly after. We had a wonderful time and a good dinner. It was all so good. My nephews found me far different than their father. Although it was late, Elsie and I stayed up to talk again.

On Monday, we had porridge for breakfast, which was our tradition at home, too. Charlie and I went for another walk down a trail at the rear of Elsie's place. Later, Elsie took us for a ride to the bank in Lockport, then out to Glenwood to see where my brother Jack had been buried. We drove the long way back to Middleport, where Elsie lived. We spent a quiet evening, just talking, relaxing and reading.

Tuesday: Go for a walk along the creek trail. Get ready for lunch. Lunch was to be at one place, which was closed that day, so we went to another little place that Nancy, Elsie's daughter who had joined us, knew.

After a light lunch, we went to the railroad museum, which was fantastic, It was also a firefighters' museum. They had about 300 firefighters' hats on shelves above the railroad and other displays. There was a miniature railroad that ran the full length of the room. It was still in the process of construction. There were all types of railroad and firefighting equipment on display. There was also a gift shop. We spent over an hour there, but could have spent more time. The members of the railroad club want to make the museum the best in the state, and I think they will succeed.

After the museum, we all went to Nancy's house for tea and pie, and to watch a video about our trip in 1994, when we visited Elsie. That was when we came for my 50-year school reunion. We spent another quiet evening at Elsie's.

Wednesday was the last day of our visit with Elsie, We went for a walk, as usual. Nancy came over to get us and drive us back, in Elsie's car, to Niagara Falls, where we would get the train back to Toronto and home again. The train came into the station, but no one got off. The station clerk told us that the train had to be inspected by customs officials. After about an hour, we were told that there was something wrong on a couple of the cars, so there would be a further delay. The clerk then asked those who were going to other places, where they had to transfer to another train for travel in Ontario, to gather their luggage, as they were to be taken to the transfer point by taxi. More people came off the train. Then, after further delay, we were informed that customs would not release the train, for some reason. We later learned that the dogs had detected drugs, or something, in one of the cars.

We were to leave the Falls at 5:45, arriving in Toronto at 7:45, but we boarded the bus that was to take us to Toronto at around 8 p.m. and arrived at 9:15. When we got on the freeway, it was almost bumper-to-bumper cars and trucks going both ways. There was no let-up in the city-to-city lights and, as we were on an express bus, there were not stops at all from Niagara Falls to Toronto. When we arrived, we went to the Royal York Hotel to get a room. It was not our normal type of hotel, but Elsie had given us the money to stay there. After much confusion about the money, we finally got a room for $109.20 + tax American. We did not have enough in Canadian funds and the girl would not accept my debit card, although she would have accepted a credit card if I had had one. We payed the charge in the American money Elsie had given us. This is something I do not understand: how some businesses will accept a credit card, when they can never be sure if the money is in the bank or not, but will not accept a debit card, when one cannot get the money unless it is in the bank.

The stay in a luxury hotel was a good ending to a wonderful visit with Elsie and her family.

A good night's rest, an early rise, breakfast in the station, and we caught the 8:30 train. We are on our way home again. There are lots of high-rise apartments, houses with very little room between them, some with hardly enough room to walk between.

I was raised in an area like that, but I could never live like that again.

The train shuffled back and forth in the train yard before leaving Toronto. There seemed to be lots of water in the lakes, streams and swamps. In Sudbury, there was more snow. It was icy outside, so I decided to stay on the train. This was the place where I had fallen before. As we were going along, it started snowing hard, and it looks like there is a blizzard brewing.

During our one-hour stop in Hornpayne, even though there was lots of snow, we were able to go for a walk to the station and back without any mishaps. Back on the train again. Charlie fell asleep and took the whole seat, so I went up to the dome car, where I had a good sleep.

It was snowing hard at Sioux Lookout, so we did not get off the train. The view from the dome car was very good. I had a front seat, where I got up on my knees for a better view. It reminded me of when I was a child: I would get on my knees to see out the back window of the car. This time, I was looking forward instead of backwards.

The construction must have been something when they were building the railroad. There must have been many marvelous feats performed to build the tunnels through the rocks like they did. There are places along the way where the tracks are right along a sheer face. Other places, the tracks go across a lake or stream on solid bridges.

We are now back in Manitoba and getting closer to home. Each click-clack of the train wheels brings us closer. We were one hour early in arriving at Winnipeg, so we had time to go for a walk to the market, where we got some fruit to eat on the train. Back to the terminal and wait for our train to depart.

As we went along, we saw our first wildlife, besides squirrels; a deer, and a flock of geese that were probably heading south to a warmer clime. The train seems to be going a lot faster now.

Saskatchewan, then Alberta, getting close and closer.

There was not enough time in Edmonton to phone Guy and Alice, another two CUSOs. A fellow on the train told us that it was thought the dog on the train at Niagara Falls had sniffed out some drugs in some of the luggage of the passengers. That is why the customs would not let the train from New York proceed. The fellow said it was common procedure for drug dealers to transport drugs across the border by train. We met lots of nice people on the train and made new friends. I sold a couple of books, too.

As we left Edmonton and were back in the mountains, we saw

more deer, a couple of moose and two or three buffalo. Some of the cattle beyond Hinton looked like beefalos (cross between buffalos and cattle). The scenery is so beautiful, so different from the prairies. This is why we call our province 'Beautiful B.C.' the Rocky Mountains are something unreal, something spectacular and hard to describe. At Jasper, another engine had been added, as well as four more cars, for our journey through the mountains. It was too dull to take pictures, which was sad, as the scenery was so great.

We both slept off and on. Then it was Hope and Mission. We were almost at the end of a wonderful trip.

Our last leg home. We arrived in Vancouver at 7:30 and had just enough time to get our bus to Powell River. The bus left at 8:15, Sunday, November 10, 2002, 21 days after we had left home.

One conclusion I have made: Canada is very beautiful, but B.C. is the most beautiful. We have learned so much about the country we live in and the people who live there. We are both happy that we had the courage to do what we did. Others should do the same. They will enjoy it as much as we did.

Cuba - 1977

In January of 1977 we went to Cuba. There had been a heavy snowfall in Powell River, which made it a good time to go on a well earned holiday. We had planned it in July and taken Spanish lessons at Malaspina College.

Cuba was my first trip to a foreign country, unless you count me as a foreigner when I lived in the United States and visited Canada as a child and young person. Charlie, of course, had been to Europe during the war. But why Cuba? It would be difficult to count the number of times my daughter, my husband or I were asked this question, from the time we first announced our intentions to take a holiday in Cuba till we left. "Why Cuba?" they would ask, and I would answer "Why not?" Each time I was asked it made me more determined to find the 'why' or 'why not' of Cuba.

My husband, Charlie, had thought of going to Cuba some years ago. Not for a holiday, but to work there. Our first decision to go to Cuba came in the Spring of 1975 when we decided to spend the next winter in a warmer place. The two previous winters had been spent in Kingston, Ontario, where we visited my grandmother, and in Kitimat when our youngest daughter had her second child. First, we decided to go to New Zealand, so went to the travel agent, only to find out that it would cost more than we could afford. In looking over the pamphlets, we came across one on Sun Tours and it included one to Cuba that interested us, so we decided then and there to go to Cuba.

In the summer of 1976 we made our reservations for January 1977. To our great pleasure, our daughter, Benita, decided to go with us. We all got passports with no trouble, got our medicals to show we were in good health and got our vaccinations in case they were needed. Charlie and I bought new summer clothes, which we needed, took Spanish lessons and started to dream of moonlight walks on the Cuban beaches.

I should say that not all the people were wondering why we

chose Cuba. There were many who were delighted and envious of us, and who thought it was a great idea. We met several people who had been there on the tours and found it to be a wonderful place with wonderful people.

Benita, Charlie and I were going to find out for ourselves what Cuba was really like. Maybe we would decide to return and stay. Who knows.

It is one week before we leave. There is still much to be done because of the time being Xmas. We still have a few things to buy (like sunglasses) and to pack. As I sit here in my dining room, I am thinking of all the comments we have heard.

From those who have been there: "It is fabulous. We really enjoyed ourselves and you will too. You can just lie on the beach, drink rum and relax."

"The accommodations are poor and the food is terrible." The last remark was from a man with lots of money, and whom no one—even the King—could satisfy.

From those who had not been there: "I envy you. It will be a wonderful trip." "Isn't that wonderful. I'm so happy for you." "I wish I could go." "I've heard it is great down there. My wife and I plan to go sometime." "Don't let them put you in jail." "Everyone there wears a green suit and has to eat, work and do exactly as the government says." "Be careful. they may not let you come back, you know." "Oh, don't go there. They are all revolutionaries and you will get mugged." "Watch that they don't take all your money."

It seems to me that the people who have been there, and know what they are talking about, say it is a great place to go. Those who have not been there, and do not really know what is truth or not truth, are against our going. Why am I going? I am going for a holiday, so I can relax and get some sunshine. I am going to see another country, which is different from mine, with different history and culture. I intend to visit the museums, parks and other areas of interest; to sit on the beaches; drink rum and do nothing. I will take walks in the moonlight, dance to the Cuban bands and enjoy myself to the utmost.

Benita is home for the Xmas holiday, but must work between Xmas and the New Year, so she will return to Kelowna and then meet us in Vancouver the night before our departure (January 3, 1977). Charlie is preparing everything at the sawmill for the closure. He is putting antifreeze in the engine, making sure the log boom is well secured, blocking off the road so that hot- rodders can't race around or steal lumber. I am home getting things ready for the trip--like the packing. Plans are now all complete. The tickets have been picked up and paid for. We have received all the information needed from our travel agent, and I think we are just about ready. The paper work is done, anyway. What does the information pamphlet say? "Tipping is prohibited, gratuities are considered demeaning." This is very good and should be practised in more places. "English is limited." Oh, oh, I should have studied my Spanish more. Oh well, I'll figure out some way to let the people know what I want (I hope). They could get the wrong idea if you are not careful how you go about it. I will worry about that when I get there. "Bar service on the plane." Goody. "Beer with meals." Goody. "Welcome cocktail party." Goody, I will try not to be drunk all the time. "Seats on first come basis." I will be in the line at 5 a.m. (ho, hum). The plane leaves at 8 a.m., but check-in is at 6 a.m. "There is no drinking water problem."

That's good. "Picture taking is restricted." We will watch it. "Bath tub plug could be missing; also toilet seat and hot water." I will take my own plug. I am used to a toilet without a seat, so this is no big deal, and I can bathe in cold water. At 80 degrees temperature, what is the difference.

We will have to make sure we have enough film, our own cosmetics, non- prescriptions, prescriptions, and other personal articles, as they may be scarce in Cuba. There will be a Cuba Tours representative to help us, at all times, with any problems we may have, which is a nice thing to know. Like the pamphlet recommends, I shall enjoy it as it is. I will go open-minded and expect to spend a peaceful, relaxing and enjoyable holiday away from the hustle and bustle of the work world.

Before going to Cuba, even though I had mentioned that I was going to, my then employer, the RCMP, when I announced that I would be leaving on January 2, the sergeant asked me if I had got permission from Ottawa. This surprised me, as I was unaware that I had to get permission to visit a communist country. I told the sergeant I felt I did not need permission and, if it meant my job, I did not care; I was going anyhow. The sergeant said he would take care of everything and I was not to worry. It was never mentioned again.

January 2, 1977–Arrival in Cuba

This is the big day. I find it hard to believe I am really going to Cuba. Charlie and I were up at 5 a.m. and caught the buss for Vancouver at 7:30. We both slept most of the way. As it was Sunday, the only places open in Vancouver were the shows, restaurants, fun arcades and the odd drug store. We went into the drug store to purchase the odd thing, like extra sun tan oil, a bath cap and some decals. After waiting 1½ hours in vain for the bus to come in from Kelowna, we went out to the airport, where the bus from the hotel picked us up. We learned, in the morning, that Benita had come on a later bus and had arrived in Vancouver about 11 p.m. She had come by bus instead of plane because of the uncertainty of the plane's departure.

The next morning, Charlie and I met Benita at the airport, where she had a roomette. After getting settled at the PWA desk, we had a glass of juice and prepared to go on the plane. We waited in the main terminal till our flight was called to go down to the departure deck. On the way, you must go through Security. Benita and I went first and had no trouble. When Charlie went through, the little red lights went on. The Security Officer stopped him and ran his little rod over him. When he ran over one of Charlie's back pockets, the buzzer went. "What is in your pocket?" Charlie reached into his back pocket and pulled out a little Crescent wrench that one of the boys had given him for Xmas and he had forgotten about. We all laughed and went on our way.

As we had been the first to get at the deck, we were the first to get our seats, which were three together on the right side of the plane. After takeoff, we were served a continental breakfast consisting of cheese, bran muffin, cinnamon bun, fruit salad and jam. Later, there were juices, a lunch which was a chicken dinner, drinks, a snack of cookies and cheese.

The weather was beautiful. The stewardesses were very helpful and the trip was most enjoyable. As one looked around, it was something to note who the people were who were travelling with us. Half the 707 plane was filled up by our group. The group consisted mostly of older people, some successful business men, and some young hippy girls, but no long-hair boys.

After six hours, with a stop for fuel in Calgary, where there was snow on the ground, we landed in Havana, Cuba. The humidity hit you even before landing. It was 24 degrees Celcius and had just stopped raining. We passed through Customs with no problems, except that a Customs officer said to Charlie, "Finis." Charlie did not understand, so prepared to open his case. The official pushed his suitcase off the desk and shouted "Finis!"

After being herded into a bus, where we got our tickets to our rooms, exchanged our money and had our passports examined by the police. We then headed for Barlovento Villa and the beach. The bus was air conditioned, with a bar in the rear. When we got our exchanged money, it was crisp new bills or pesos in an envelope. The police had come on the bus to examine the passports, because there were one too many people there. On the way to Barlovento or Varadaro Beach, we saw very little, as it was so dark, but what we did see intrigued me. The bus ride was a long one, but cervaza (beer) helped pass the time.

At Barlovento Villa, we got our keys to our room, collected our luggage and went to our room to clean up. We then went to supper.

After, Benita went to bed while Charlie and I took a walk on the beach.

Each villa had a housekeeper to look after the place and give you any help you might need. Our housekeeper, named Georgina, was a real pearl. She kept our place spotless and gave us all the help we needed. She did not speak English, but we were able to communicate very well. There was also a Negro fellow who swept the street every day. He was an older man, but was very healthy. He complained a lot, but was very cheerful about it. In Cuba, if you can work, you do. If you cannot, the government looks after you. You work according to your ability and get paid according to your need. There was no unemployment in Cuba. this was in 1977 and I do not know how it is today.

Tuesday, January 4 - First Day

Charlie and I had breakfast in the common eating area and then went for a walk while Benita slept. Then Benita and I went while Charlie slept. There was a ten o'clock meeting where we were told what we could do and what we could not do. It was advisable not to wander too far on your own, because of the language problem.

Tipping is prohibited, also selling anything to Cubans. If we were caught selling, we would be a guest of the Cuban Government for about a year, and there was nothing Sun Tours or the Canadian Government could do. Buying from someone selling, except in a store or such, was also prohibited.

Charlie and I went to Varadaro City in the afternoon. To our disappointment, we were asked to buy a shell by a young fellow who stopped us in the park. We arrived back just in time to clean up for supper, which was "Cuba Night Supper." After this we danced to a live band and then went to bed.

Wednesday, January 5 - Bike Ride to Varadaro

Up late. Breakfast. Then Charlie and I went for a bike ride while Benita stayed on the beach with Vickie, who was also from Powell

River and had gone to school with Benita. They had met on the plane by surprise. It was nice for both of them, as there were not many other young people on the tour. Charlie and I had a ball on the bike, which was a tandem. We went first for a ride along the road. We stopped to read a sign. Cars beeped at us and we figured out the sign meant "No step on grass," and there we were, bicycle and all. On the way back to the house, the truck stops. We keep going. The truck beeps and shows us the sign that says "Stop," which we have just driven through.

We peddled on to Varadaro, where we stopped at a beer stand and met several people, including two Russians. The fellow serving at the stand told us much about the Cuban schools, prisons and other things of interest. Students go to school for the first six years in a grade school, then four years in a high school and four years in a pre-university school. If they wish, and if they have the intelligence, they go free to university to take a course of their choice. English is compulsory in Grades 8-10. In the prisons, which are really farms, the prisoners work for their keep, but also receive a small remuneration. There are no bars or fences. The dangerous prisoners, like murderers, etc, are kept in a prison with a fence. If you steal, or commit some minor offense, you go to the farm. We asked the fellow who was serving why there were no policemen around, as we had never seen one. He told us, "We police each other. See that fellow over there. If he saw me short change you, he would come over here and tell me to give you the right change. We need no policemen here, except for the really bad guys." The only time we ever saw or heard of a policeman coming to the resort was when a woman reported her watch stolen, and the thief proved to be another person in the same villa as she was.

The afternoon was spent on a tour to the caves, which proved interesting, but was uneventful. We went way underground and were told some funny tales, like the one about a certain spring that was the fountain of youth. Another that "In this spring you can bathe, but remember that a beautiful girl bathed in it and then disappeared."

As we were very tired, we went to bed after supper. Benita and

Vickie went to the "Pirates' Cave," a night club. In the afternoon, we had all met a singer from there. The girls, with two Cubans, really enjoyed themselves.

Thursday, January 6 - Rodeo

Morning on the beach. One moment, a fellow who was there said he was in university studying immigration and then, later, tried to buy our radio, which he knew was against the law. As Charlie had wanted to work in Cuba, this might have been one way, except that he might find himself in a sugar field working, instead of running machinery. In the afternoon, we went to a rodeo, which was very good. The events were run one after another with no delays and no prizes given out. The only disappointment was that they charged us two pesos at the motel and admission at the gate was only one peso. We noticed this before, that they charged the tourists more. When we were in PNG we noticed this also. Russians paid one-half less than Canadians did. This is the only thing I found wrong with Cuba: A few Cubans thought us to be big Canadians who could buy anything and could give them things because we could always buy more. It is pure garbage, the belief that people have that you cannot mix with the people, or that you will only be allowed to see what they want you to see—only the good things. Charlie and I travelled as we chose and where we chose. No one restricted us. The only restriction was that we were not allowed inside the school grounds without permission. In Canada this is true too. The schools here do not want people wandering around the school. This is understandable. We have met many people so far, and all of them are very friendly. However, like in Canada and other places, if you befriend some, they will expect a favor from you. I find Cuba no different from Canada. They are just a little poorer, but they are working hard to improve this. Everywhere you go, you see improvements in housing, etc. The people are not dressed in fancy clothes like us, but they are dressed well. Their food and clothing is on ration, but free. They get so much each week, and more if they work more. With this extra money, they can buy radios, televisions, etc. This is no different, in a way, than us. The fellow who works more gets more.

After supper, which was not too bad, we walked on the beach, had a couple of drinks and went to bed. There was entertainment every night, but we did not join in. Benita and Vickie did.

Friday, January 7 - Bay of Pigs; Crocodile Farm; Guama

Up early to catch bus for Bay of Pigs. The driver spoke very good English and was very good looking. He told us lots about the revolution which I do not want to repeat here, as I do not have the exact dates or names, and besides, the history of Cuba can be read in any encyclopedia and has been written in many books. The following are some notes which I did take on the way to the Bay of Pigs.

The main industry of Cuba is sugar. Before the revolution, the U.S. used the Cubans to grow the sugar. Then they shipped the raw sugar to the States, where it was refined, and sold it back to the Cubans at big prices. (This sounds very familiar.) Now the sugar is refined in Cuba and the people have sugar for the first time. Before, the people could not afford to buy their own sugar which they had grown.

Varadaro Beach, which is one of the most beautiful beaches in the world, was out of bounds for the Cuban people, as were many of the beaches. The rich Cubans and the Americans owned most of the beaches, if not all of them before. Now, Cubans of all classes can enjoy the beaches. The Cuban people are all equal. The one thing the people were extremely happy about was the fact that they could go to the beaches whenever they wanted to.

Rope is their second industry. Some is still harvested by hand, as is the sugar cane, but most then, and probably, as I write this, is by machine. We passed a chicken farm. The chickens had come from Canada, and the driver told us they are very conscientious chickens. They lay three eggs a day: one for breakfast, one for lunch and one for supper. We also passed a beautiful cemetery, where each grave had a stone. This is not always true here in Canada anymore, and I wonder if it has changed in Cuba Too.

Here is a joke we heard in Vardero: The Inspector was inspecting the school and asked one of the students, "Peter, where is the Sierra Madre?"

Peter answered, "I did not take them, Senor Madre?"

The Inspector said to the teacher, "Did you hear what that boy said? He said he did not take the Sierra Madre."

"Well, if the boy says he did not take them, he did not take them."

The inspector went to the principal of the school and told him what the pupil and teacher had said.

The principal said, "Close the doors till they find the Sierra Madre. I do not want to be a witness."

Back to the bus ride. The driver told us that Cuba is the same as any other country; there are good Cubans and bad Cubans. In all countries, there are nice people and there are terrible people. After the revolution, Castro told the people, "If you want to go, you can go." Many people did leave, because they did not like the system. Before the revolution, and under Batista, if the people said, "I do not like Batista. I do not like his system, or his government, the people would be put in prison, tortured and killed. Now, if you do not like the system, you can say so, but, like in Canada, you must still obey the rules and regulations. You are free to go as you want. People here are proud of their country.

Cadina, one of the rural cities we passed through, is a port and an agriculture town, the only one in Cuba. It was noted that the housing was very poor but comfortable. In Cuba, a group of people or workers get together and build an apartment house. Then the poor people with poor houses can get an apartment. Cubans are trying to rid the cities of poor houses by building new houses, repairing old houses and painting others. Some houses are torn down and replaced by new houses or apartments, or built into a park. Cuba has many parks. Apartments are free to the people and are furnished.

After the men are finished school, including university if they choose, they must serve three years in the military. This is not compulsory for the women, but they can serve if they wish. Many of the men have more than one job. While in the military, they get military training, but also must study. In the school system, which the Cubans are very proud of, the primary students live at home and go to school each day the same as we do, or they can attend a boarding school. The high school students, however, are housed in a school on a farm or plantation, where they attend school half the day and work the other half. University is the same. Students can go home every weekend if they choose. They attend school Monday through Friday one week, with a full week end; the next week they work half a day on Saturday. All education, meals and room are free. Students also receive a small sum for their work. There are many schools. From Grade 8 up, the students not only learn Spanish, but English and Russian. Many here speak these three languages and French as well.

The sugar cane is planted in the spring and harvested from November to January. After 15 years of growing, or if they become diseased, the canes are burnt and new plants are planted. We passed a railroad and were surprised to see the ties were made of concrete, with iron rails. This is one transportation system which is being improved. Before, it took 24 hours to get from one end of the Island to the other. It is hoped, when the new system is finished, that the trip will be made by a faster train in only eight hours. I would like to make the trip in the future.

As you speak to some of the people who were there before the revolution, you find the same old story: The U.S. moves in with their big money, takes over and does what they want. The people become slaves to them. I only hope Canadians do not spoil it for themselves by acting big, giving gifts and acting superior to the Cuban people. We have noticed some of this, and the Cuban Government does not want it.

We went to a crocodile farm where there was one crocodile that was 100 years old. The crocodiles are used to make shoes, purses, etc., and the meat is eaten by the Cubans. On the farm there were 9.000 crocodiles. They produced 304 eggs a year each.

One thing I noticed, that I have never seen in Canada, is goats grazing in a field. There probably are some, but I never noticed them like I did in Cuba.

We stopped by a three-trunked palm tree, the only one in Cuba, and we noticed four students goofing off the same as they do in Canada. The students work by themselves. There is nobody standing over them to see that they work. Many would like to be home with their parents more often.

Our tour of the Bay of Pigs was good, but we missed going to sugar cane fields and getting sugar cane. We also missed seeing the main part of Guama, which is an ancient Indian village, because some people spent too much time buying trinkets, etc. from the small store there. We were served, as we had been every day, a very good lunch. Another delay on the trip happened when our boat ran out of gas on the way to the Indian village. We had gone by boat because the village was on an island in the middle of a lake. This village once had many natives, but the Spanish killed them all. Our driver told us the story of the Bay of Pigs, and it was not a pretty story. However, the Cubans are proud they ousted the Americans. One Cuban said, "We don't need those people. We have friends in Russia." It was noticed that the Cubans cater to socialist country people. The people are convinced that socialism is the only system because they can see what socialism has done for them and how it has changed their lives for the better. There is a group for the younger generation in the Communist Party, but not until you are 27 do you become a full-fledged member of the party, and you remain such till you are 60. It must be mentioned that many of the people do not like to be called a communist. They say they are 'Social Democrats.' The people of the socialist countries get their goods, etc. cheaper than Canadians do. Many Russians go to Cuba for their vacations. The Cubans can only visit socialist countries. They work for six months and get two weeks holidays.

At Barloventa, near where we stayed, the Villa is used for tourists from December to April. Then the Cubans use it for their vacations. The people are well fed, well clothed, and live in comfortable homes. There are no long-hairs in Cuba. The men are all neat and trim. To our surprise, the men do not wear beards as was supposed. Green suits. Yes, some men are in green suits, but they are the military.

We noticed many cars of the late 1950s. There are no 'hot rods' and all the cars have quiet mufflers. The only noisy things on the streets are the air brakes of the trucks. Not all the people have cars, but many do. You can work extra and then purchase a car. You must work and earn enough. There are no daddies to buy it for you.

The people have televisions too. This country is really developing and moving ahead. The people are friendly and all are willing to help you with anything, especially with the language. (This was in 1977. The people are still very friendly, but, by reports, the country is suffering from the embargoes by the U.S.)

Friday night found me sicker than I had been for a long time. There were several people sick, with pains in their stomachs and diarrhea, but as far as I know, I was the only one who threw up. Saturday was spent in bed. On Sunday I went to the hospital to receive treatment and get some medicine (which was free). The rest of Sunday was spent in bed too. In the evening we met a pharmacist who gave me some tablets to take and much advice as to eating, so that on Monday I was much better. I think it was the lobster, as I have since discovered that I cannot eat it without getting ill. We spent most of Monday walking on the beach and went for a long bicycle ride. In the evening a wind came up, but it was lovely out and I sat on the porch of our villa and wrote part of this story. Benita and her friend, Vickie, had been doing Okay. One night they went to a night club with two Cubans. another day they went golfing. Today they went for a car ride with the Sunflight Rep. Tonight, a group from Ottawa, who are leaving tomorrow, are having a farewell party in one of the other villas. I still have pains in my stomach, but am feeling much better. Tomorrow we are going to Havana.

When we were at the caves and were waiting for some people to come out, I went to the "Dames" room. It was a square brick building: four walls with a small door, no roof or windows, and a cement floor with a hole in the middle. this was a surprise to me and later, when I got sick, I was thankful for our modern bathroom. In our villa we had a modern bathroom with a toilet and a spigot, which is a European toilet with a small tap in the center that gives a spray of water to wash your bum.

Tuesday, January 11 and Wednesday, January 12 - Havana

Havana. Along the way to Havana we stopped at one of the many housing developments, the La Mar, which houses about 1600 people. It is to be one of the largest housing developments in Cuba. The people only pay 10 percent of their wages for rent. Cuba is trying to get the people out of their poor housing and into better facilities.

We visited one museum before going to our hotel. The Cubans are very proud of their success in the revolution and seem to be content with the system they live under. We had visited a cemetery too. It was the most beautiful cemetery I had ever seen. The monuments were made of marble. Everyone is buried here free and all are entitled to a marble stone. Families are buried together, often in the same tomb.

Havana is a city different from any city I have ever visited. There is a great contrast from buildings which were built in the 18th century to ones which were built in only the last few years. The Capri Hotel is a very modern building and stands among some very, very old Spanish buildings. Some of the people live in nice housing developments, but others live in very shabby houses. However, the houses may be shabby on the outside, but inside there is nice furniture with modern fixtures, a television and a fridge. The urban people are very friendly and everyone greets you with "good day." We stayed in the National Hotel, a very old hotel with modern furniture—except the toilet seat. Most toilets in Cuba do not have a seat, and very often the door is missing on public toilets.

Our room in the hotel was absolutely gorgeous. It was actually a suite, with a sofa, chairs and coffee table. There were two beautiful maple dressers with a large-size bed to match. I have never slept in a room like it. It was very similar to the royal suite in the Empress Hotel in Victoria. There was a full bathroom with tub and shower. There were deep red velvet drapes on the windows and a pile rug on the floor. Benita and Vickie were not so lucky and had a much simpler room. They were jealous of us. It was sure a luxurious experience. In the evening we were entertained at the Tropicabanna Night Club. The show was absolutely spectacular. The theme of the show was "Cuba for Everyone." It featured dances and songs from many countries. The costumes were so beautiful. It was a continual show on a stage that was circular and was divided into three parts. The stage went around, showing first one performance, then another and then a third. During the show they served us drinks and snacks. It was wonderful. The next day Charlie and I wandered around the streets of Havana on our own and no one bothered us, except some young kids who were always asking for "Chicolets." Their English at that age was not as good as the older children's: they always said 'Good-bye' instead of 'Hello.' Benita and Vickie went to the University with some students they had met the day before. Many of the old buildings in Havana are being torn down to make room for better housing facilities for the people. Others are being repaired, the same as is being done all over the country. There is much land in Cuba that is still not being used. All the arable land is put in agriculture. Housing and industry are built on the barren land. The livestock graze on the rope fields, orchards and other fields. This gives fields a double use.

Whether it was the water, the bus ride, or what, Thursday found me sick to my stomach again. The food of Cuba just does not seem to agree with me. The girls were invited to dinner with a Cuban family. They are getting around very well and getting to know the people. They have met those who are not completely content with Cuba. One was a fellow whose family left for the States in 1961 when Castro told the people "Anyone who wants to go can go." This fellow's parents were Americans. He decided to stay and now he cannot get out. Another fellow was a Jamaican and he decided to live here. Now he cannot immigrate anywhere but in a socialist country. Benita met a soldier who had been in Angola and wanted to go to Florida because his parents and girl friend were there. It seems his parents left Cuba after the revolution, when he was a baby, and left him behind. Maybe they could not take him. There does seem to be much that a person does not understand. The people do not talk too much about their politics.

Friday-Sunday, January 14-16 - Going Home Again

A day to lie on the beach, getting all the Cuban sunshine we can get. In the afternoon we went to the Dupont Estates, with all the evidence of a rich American family, which the Cuban people had to cater to. We were stopped from going down a certain road and, later, discovered that this was where the Russians were staying. We saw the villa that had been built for them alone. In the evening we watched the fishermen along the canal, fishing with lamps and nets.

On Saturday we rented bicycles and went to the next town. As we approached one road by a sugar cane field, a soldier jumped out with gun and bayonet in hand and shook his finger at us. We changed our minds about going down this road. It was the road to a military establishment.

On another road, we came to a machine shop, where we talked with the men and Charlie looked over the machines they were repairing. We found that with a little effort on each one's part we could understand each other. The people in the town were like those all over Cuba, friendly. One man told us he was going to school part-time, learning to be an architect. He told us that in Cuba one can learn anything he wants and the opportunity is there to learn free.

In the evening, the people of Varlovento, where we stayed, had another of their 'Fiesta de Mar' parties. There was a good band and lots of food and drink. Everyone had a wonderful time. Charlie and I took a walk. We felt sorry that soon we would be leaving this quiet and relaxing Cuba and returning to the hustle and bustle of work.

On Sunday the sky was overcast and the sea roared. We learned there had been a terrible storm in the Southern States and their crops had been frozen. The day before (Saturday), when we were on our way back from the small town we had gone to, after bicycling up and down several roads, we came to another road we thought led to the canal. There was a gravel pit where a dragline was dredging the sand from the canal and a loader was loading it into trucks bound for where we did not know. The man on the loader came down from his machine during an intermission of the trucks, dug into the sand piles and gave me some shells he had found. Charlie and I went to a bank away from the working area and found some more shells.

The day we left, we felt a bit sad to leave our new-found friends. The people had been so good to us that, in a way, we regretted leaving. But duty calls. Charlie was not feeling too good and, on the plane, he was sick. When we arrived in the Vancouver airport, he had to go to the restroom while the others went through Customs. This made Charlie and me the last ones to go through and, as it was late, the Customs officials were anxious to go home. They hustled us through and it was a good thing they did not open my suitcase and search it, as the man may have cut his hand. The bottle of rum I bought before leaving had broken. We had decided to go to the Truck Loggers' Convention before going home. When we got to our hotel I discovered the broken bottle of rum. My clothes were all soaked in rum. Charlie said, "Never mind. The men will never notice. Most of them will smell the same."

I cleaned the glass out of my suitcase and hung my clothes in the bathroom to dry. I don't know what the housekeeper thought when she came to clean up our room the next morning. She probably was used to strange things happening.

After a good time at the convention, we went home with many memories of a wonderful holiday. Friends of ours went to Cuba last year (1996). They said it was the best holiday they ever had. The people were so friendly and seemed to be the same as when we were there.

St. Marc, Haiti–An Experience–1987

Boy, was it hot there! As members of Communities in Partnership, Charlie and I had the pleasure of personally meeting, and making friends with, several Haitians when they visited their twin city, here in Powell River.

First to come was Francious Bergome, the mayor of St. Marc, who came in August 1986. Then, in September 1988, Charles Edwarzie, St. Marc's postmaster and coordinator of L'Alliance, the equivalent of CIP there. In July 1987, Miss Powell River-St. Marc came, with her chaperones, to take part in the Powell River Pageant and visit Powell River. CIP, along with the Farmers' Institute, hosted 15 pig farmers from St. Marc in August 1987.

Charlie and I, with other Powell Riverites, had sponsored students and had pen pals in St. Marc. Others had made a trip to Haiti to see their pen pals and students, as well as friends we had made when they visited. So Charlie and I decided to take the trip, too. We wanted to visit the girl we sponsored and visit the boy who was our pen pal. We also wanted to visit the many friends we had made before.

Have you ever spent a night in the Vancouver Airport? The chairs are hard to sit in, let alone try to sleep in. In 1982, when we spent a night in that airport, there were soft chairs that you could cuddle up in, but no more. The rooms that were available then are no longer there either. The seats were being used by undesirables and the rooms were being used by hookers; so both were eliminated. Another case of the comforts of the general public being spoiled by a few.

After a good breakfast and lunch on the plane, we found ourselves at Dorval Airport, where we had to take a bus to the Marabel Airport and a $86 per night room. Wow! What a place–a swimming pool and a classy restaurant (we did not eat there). There were lots of gardens to wander around in, too.

Up early. After a swim, we are on the plane and off to Port au-Prince, Haiti, where we are met by Charles, St. Marc's postmaster. After we were settled in where we were to stay, we were whisked off to a party at Francious Bergome's (by then, former mayor), where we met our pen pal Harry, and our sponsored student, Erline, as well as the pig farmers we had met when they visited Powell River. Here, as in the days to follow, there was a great feast prepared for us by the women of the group and their neighbors. It was unbelievable–the amount of food, rice and beans, salads of all kinds, beef, pork and goat meat, sometimes chicken, macaroni and rice dishes of every description. The food would cover a table 10-14 feet long. There were anywhere from 20 to 80 people there to greet us with hand-shaking and hugs, til you thought your arms would fall off.

In the two weeks we were in Haiti, there were between 10 and 20 people escorting two people around St. Marc. In Powell River, one or two people escorting fifteen people. St. Marc–50 to 150 people at a meeting—Powell River, 15-20 people. Why?

A Toronto Agency, Canadian Foundation for World Develpment (CFWD), has a house in St. Marc for Canadians, and others, who come for a visit or to work in Haiti. This is where Charlie and I stayed. It is run by Louise, a 25-year old girl from Calgary who is dedicated to the development of Haiti, especially the St. Marc area. She starts at 7 a.m., getting ready for her activities of the day and getting Anius ready for school. Anius is a six-year old boy who fell into a boiling pot of beans at the age of four and was severely burned. A Canadian doctor discovered him about a year-and-a-half ago, living in the mountains above St. Marc. The doctor made arrrangements for Anius to go to Sarnia, Ontario for treatment. Anius returned to Haiti, where Louise took him into her care.

Louise is involved with many other CFWD projects in Haiti, such as clinics, schools, workshops and tree planting. Communities in Partnership began with the help of this organization and continues to operate on their projects in Haiti with the help of CFWD.

On our first Sunday, we went to the Catholic Church with our pen pal, Harry and our student, Erline. We had not learned French, even though Josie Cross had tried to teach us, and Jack Anderson did his best to try to teach us Creol. We needed an interpreter. So Lesard, who had been assigned to this job, met us at the church, which was packed with people singing. The sermon was in session when we entered.

We were led to the front of the church, where Lesard made the girls in the choir move over and make room for us on the bench. Talk about embarrassment! There were about 300 or more people watching. During the sermon, the people in the church sang a song of welcome to us.

After church, we visited a young girl involved with L'Alliance (CIP in St. Marc), who had broken her leg in an accident.

This brings to mind the traffic in St. Marc: busses, pick-ups, and trucks loaded with bags of rice, chickens and everything you can imagine, piled as high as possible. And there were people sitting on top of that, and others crammed inside the vehicles like sardines. They travel down the narrow roads, right through the center of town, at speeds of 40-to-80 miles per hour without slowing down for anyone. They just lean on the horn and continue on. The people just step aside and do not seem to object. There are no traffic regulations. It is absolutely unbelievable. As one can imagine, there are many people killed and injured each year, but surprisingly less than one might expect. Every time we drove anyplace, I hung onto my seat and prayed., Sometimes, I was surprised that we made it without hitting another vehicle or a person on the road. We have some crazy drivers in Powell River, but we're no comparison to St. Marc.

Sunday night we met with the group from L'Alliance and made plans for the coming week, which proved to be very busy and unforgettable.

Monday was a day of visits. The Mayor, the Prefect (the government representative), the post office, the wharf, the Captain of the Army, the Agriculture Minister, the fire and water department, and the radio station. There were discussions on how we, in Powell River, could help them. The lights in Louise's house were out; so she took us to a local restaurant for supper.

On Tuesday we went out to visit a pig farm that belonged to one of the men who had visited Powell River. It was a well-kept farm with cement stalls and facilities for 300 pigs. Marc, the vet, did a castration operation on two of the big pigs. Seeing this was, in itself, an experience. I was right in there, watching the whole process.

In the evening, we were taken to meet a youth group, where we were given gifts and a local band played for us.

Wednesday, Thursday and Friday, Charlie went to a couple of other farms (one was 20 miles square), to the local hospital and several government departments. I did not go because I was sick in bed. Whether it was, sunstroke or just the same old dysentery that everyone else gets sooner or later, we did not know. It sure had been hot at Roger's farm on Tuesday. There were no worries about the water or the food, at least where we went.

On Friday, Harry, our pen pal came over after school and we went up to see his house, which was a bit different from the ones we had seen on our organized visit. His mother served us a cold Coke, which is the standard drink in St. Marc and, probably, in all of Haiti.

I might mention the house construction, which was 80 percent, or more, of concrete. Many houses had a type of design in the bricks or slabs, even on the ceiling. Also, many houses had colored cement–pink, lime green and other beautiful colors, with some works of art here and there.

The people of St. Marc were neat and clean in their dress and in their homes. Many had very little, but what they had, they looked after. However, the streets were appalling. They were cluttered and dirty. The sewer runs along the edge of the road, and it stinks.

We were fed like royalty, but we wondered, 'Will they suffer for this?' Many parents are struggling to find the money to send their children to school, but do not have the money to feed them properly. A common complaint is 'I cannot see the blackboard.' This is because they have not had enough to eat and are undernourished. Haiti is one of the poorest countries in the world. We saw only a little evidence of this, but we knew it was there.

Every night, there were lightning storms–no rain, but thunder and lightning. It was neat to watch, especially at about 2 a.m.

All night long, we would hear the transport trucks and busses go by. Some had musical horns. I thought them neat, or 'awesome,' as they say today, but Charlie did not. Neither did Louise, or the other girl at the house, who had listened to them for some time. I thought it would be great to get one for our son's logging truck, but Charlie convinced me that people in Powell River would not appreciate it. Neither would my son.

On Saturday, we witnessed another operation by Marc. It was a small pig that had a hernia. When he was smaller, his mother had stepped on him.

We were to go to a youth and communal forest, but, for some reason, we did not go. We did go to a forestry place, a week later, on our way to the airport.

On our second Sunday, we went to the Baptist Church, which was also crowded. The church means a lot to the people of St. Marc. Several people came up to the front of the church and spoke, including us. After the sermon and singing, a politician in the upcoming election came up from the front of the church, waving his pamphlet, and gave a speech to the people. A collection was taken for him. Then the administrator of the church came up and talked to the people about the responsibility of getting out and voting. Politics in a church was a new thing for us.

After church and a feast at the Ketleys' (the lady in the agriculture department) we visited the home of our school sponsor-girl, where we had another feast. We got to meet her parents and the rest of the family at this time. In the evening, we had visits from the fishermen and a youth group.

On both Monday and Tuesday, we were supposed to go to the Baihi School, but there was some difficulty getting transport and the road to the place was not too good. So, unfortunately, we were unable to go. Charlie and I went to town and phoned home, walked on the beach and generally rested these days. It gave us a chance to see the countryside by ourselves.

Wednesday: We had the pleasure of going to see the Albert Switzer Hospital. It was a unique hospital with all the modern equipment. It was not the same as our hospitals, but excellent for

Haiti. It was better than any of the hospitals in Papua New Guinea, where the white people were given good treatment and good beds, but the dark, or local, people slept on mats on the floor or on bare beds.

The Switzer Hospital had a workshop where furniture was made for the hospital or to be sold outside. There was a ceramic shop, where the dishes, etc. for the hospital were made, as well as a gift shop. The hospital grew its own food and had a chicken farm. Cows, horses, pigs and goats were raised to supply the hospital or to be sold. They had a program in which they gave a farmer a pig and, when the pig had a litter, the farmer repaid the hospital for the pig he had received with a pig from the litter. The hospital also had a tree nursery, where they grew trees for the farmers to plant. The place was absolutely self-sustaining.

Besides the hospital and a clinic, there was a veterinarian clinic where people could bring their sick animals for treatment.

Thursday and Friday were run-around days, with visits to Miss St. Marc, Joselyn and others. On Friday, we went swimming for the first time, and it was great. On the way to the beach, we stopped at one of the few tourist hotels in Haiti. Friday was also our day for packing to go home. In the evening, there was a 'farewell party for Charlie and Gerri,' at which time, the certificates from Powell River to the pig farmers were given out.

Saturday, on our way back to Porta Au Prince, we visited the one pig farm that we had not visited before. Then we paid a visit to the Double Harvest Agro-Forestry Project. Several people came to see us off.

Porta Au Prince–35 degrees. Montreal–4 degrees and windy. What a difference. We had a day between planes. So we boarded a bus and went down into the city (Montreal). Boy, was it ever windy. I nearly got blown off the sidewalk. After stopping in a restaurant for a cup of tea, we walked around until we saw an advertisement for a city bus tour outside a bus station. We decided to take the tour.

One of the stops on the tour was at Notre Dame Church, which was one of the most spectacular sights I have ever seen. It was just beautiful, with all the gold fixtures and statues. We enjoyed the tour very much. The stonework on some of the buildings was fantastic.

Most of the tour was in the old part of Montreal. The bus went up the mountain to the Mount Royal Lookout, where we could view the city below.

After the tour, we went to another bus station, where we waited for our bus back to the airport.

Home again. Would I go again? No, I would not go again. But I have no regrets that we did go. The people of St. Marc are wonderful, but the traffic, poverty and corruption were hard to take.

Two Tickets on the E&N - 1990

Some time ago, our friend Norma took her girls for a trip on the E&N Railroad from Courtenay to Victoria. We thought, then, that we would like to make the trip ourselves. Years later, when there was the threat of losing the railroad, we decided to do it. We were not alone; many others thought the same thing.

On short notice, the day before New Years 1990, we checked the schedule, reserved a motel room in Victoria and were off with our back packs to catch the train in Courtenay. We caught the 9:15 ferry to Vancouver Island, had breakfast on the ferry and went to the train station, where we met a girl with a baby. We all went to Bino's, in town, for lunch, then back to the train station to wait for the train.

There is no problem catching the train if you take the 9:15 ferry from Powell River. It is best to travel light–a day to Victoria and a day back. We spent two nights in a nice motel for only $30 a night.

On the way to Victoria, we had one stop for 15 minutes, in Nanaimo, where we got a cup of coffee and a rest. It was raining in Victoria; so we took a taxi to the motel. We got settled in, then went out for a Chinese meal and back to the motel to watch TV.

We found lots to do in Victoria, even on New Year's Day-the one day of the year when the Provincial Museum is closed. The weather should never be a problem, if you dress for it. Of course, going without wheels, you have to take the city busses, which are nice and warm, and "you see more, looking out the side windows, than you see through the windshield" (Charlie's comment).

Different people see different things. Charlie sees the development, or the lack of it; the ever-changing movie tells one many things: the work and investment that people have put into the land; the old run-down shacks and the beautiful homes, barns and fields; construction buildings and equipment all along the way; the utilization and the waste; the opportunities taken and many more waiting.

The railroad needs repair or better upkeep. The trees along the route are getting taller; so you travel through a tunnel of trees that should be thinned and branched. There are millions of Christmas trees that could provide jobs. There is some selective logging being done, and there are mountains of wood slash being burned that could be turned into particle board, or hog fuel to generate electricity.

Some people want to dump the railroad; others want to keep it but, let's face it, the railroad has problems. We passed only one level loading platform. There is no baggage car. Trucks haul the heavy freight and curriers haul the packages. The E&N hauls only people, but the two-car train was full at Nanaimo. Some people use the train regularly, many are first-timers like us, but everyone seems to enjoy it, especially the kids. The railroad helped to build the Island communities and the E&N had a good thing, with the land grant and all. Today, it should belong to the people. It is a heritage thing that should be kept alive. We have lost so much of the days of the steam engine. It would be a shame to shut the railroad down.

The above are comments from Charlie on the trip. Now a few from Gerri as to our time in Victoria:

New Year's Day 1990

We arose later than we had anticipated. It was a short walk to the bus stop-we caught it half-way across a bridge. We went first to the train station to get our tickets for the trip back to Courtenay. As it was a holiday, many of the restaurants were closed and we had a hard time finding a place to eat. We walked around, went through the conference centre and the lobby of the Empress Hotel. We went into the wax museum, which was scary, and into the undersea gardens. Lots of the places were closed. We took a walk up Douglas Street, where we had tea and pie in a small café. Then we took the Yates Street bus, went to the end of the line, walked around a park, and the Gorge, then back to our motel. Chinese food again, in the Wings Restaurant. Got some milk at a local store and went back to the motel, where we had baths and watched TV.

The next day, we were up early and went by bus to the train station. After having coffee at the A&W, we boarded the train at 8:15. We stopped again in Nanaimo and were soon back in Courtenay, where we went to Canadian Tire and a trade store before catching the 3 p.m. ferry to Powell River.

Now that we have the hang of backpacking, we want to do more of it.

A Trip down Under-1990

The day we had been waiting for was here at last.

After a trip on the bus, down the same old winding road, we arrived at the Vancouver Bus Station just as the Airport Express Bus pulled in. It took us on a trip around town, to several hotels, to pick up other passengers, then over Oak Street Bridge and on to the airport, where we arrived four hours early.

After a couple of snack breaks, rest stops and walks, we boarded the plane for New Zealand. There was some delay on the take-off due to some problem concerning a couple with a child. No explanation was given. Drinks, dinner, sherbet and juice on the plane, in the holding area at Honolulu Airport, and we were off again, on the third leg of our trip.

Arrival: 7 a.m. Sunday, April 1, 1990, having lost a day in crossing the international date line. There was a beautiful moon shining as we went through the customs with no problem. A bus was waiting to take us to the Leisure Post, where we picked up the mini-van we would be travelling in. It was a really nice van, with fridge, stove and all the necessities of comfort. We were all set to go adventuring. It took Charlie a while to learn the different gears and the clutch, as well as driving on the left side of the road (even though he had driven like that when we were in P.N.G. with CUSO). We drove around a hotel parking lot to get some practice, then read our maps, etc. to find out where we were and where we wanted to go.

The first stop was a small café to get a cup of tea, which cost us $3.50 each, as there was a cover charge. Travelling on the Motorway (freeway in Canada), we went to Drury, where we located the Husqvarna Shop and visited a man whom Charlie wanted to see about a special saw tooth for the Forestry Museum in Powell River.

We had had enough of the freeway traffic, so headed out on Route 22, a back road. It was good most of the way, but a little bit rough for the last bit. Stopping at the B.P. Store in Paerata, we got a quart of milk and some jam to eat with the buns we had saved from our meal on the plane. We ate these beside the Wakora River.

Down a side road, over a bridge spanning the Wakora River and down another side road, where we bought some fruit and vegetables at a farm store and viewed a deer farm. On the road, there were lots of dead animals that had been hit by cars, but there were lots of live sheep and cows, too. We had to stop every once-in-a-while to find out where we were, as there were lots of junctions on the road. Coming to a rest stop, created by local students, we enjoyed a lovely bush walk. However, there were no toilet facilities, the one thing we found missing at rest stops on our trip.

After travelling about 30 km, we hit Route 23 and headed for Hamilton on a road with no more winding turns. At our first gas (oops! I should say 'petrol') stop, in Cambridge, we got some instructions and more groceries. Cambridge was a small town, where we located a pleasant spot under a bridge to camp for the night. We were so tired that we fell asleep as soon as our heads hit the pillow. In the morning, we went for a walk around the site, where we noticed bear tracks from an unknown visitor in the night. Further down a trail, we came upon a tree with a cable through it and another tree that had grown over a cable that had been wrapped around it.

Pack up our gear, and we are on our way again down the road. We pass another deer farm and see one of the biggest pigs I have ever seen, big bulls, too, and lots of big and little sheep. Food is fairly expensive here. Instead of 'take-outs,' they have 'take-aways.' It was surprising how much their money was the same as that in P.N.G. The people of New Zealand are so friendly. At a small café, we had a good clean-up in the washroom. Some people would call the washrooms primitive, but I found them adequate. They were like luxury out-houses with runing water–cold, but running–and a flush toilet (button on the top of the tank, like P.N.G.). We found the drivers were not as courteous as in Canada, especially the truckers.

Our next stop was Tauaanga, where we got some ice cream and walked around the shopping center. We had been warned, early, to be aware of some people; so we steered clear of one man who looked suspicious to us.

On our way again. Stopped at a Historic Village, where we had an interesting walk among old trains and cars, as well as engines and other machinery. As we were not sure where we were going, we asked some people for advice.

Over the years, New Zealand had cut most of their forests; so now they are reforesting thousands of acres. There are places where you cannot see the end of the tree plantations. Farmers are planting trees where, once, they had cut the trees down for pasture.

After a big downpour, we saw, for the first time, two beautiful rainbows at once. They seemed to come right out of the ground.

Our second night's stop was at the Fern Leaf Motel in Rotorura. The owners of the motel were the brother and sister-in-law of John Bloxham of Powell River. John and his brother Stuart had not seen each other for 30 years. While in Rotorua, we visited the Forest

Industry Centre, where, like the centre in P.N.G., the students learn about forestry by hands-on experience. The centre started out with a working sawmill, but has advanced into tree planting, logging, forestry research, marketing and forest management. It is something we need in Canada. Charlie and I have had the idea for some time. Powell River would be an ideal spot.

While we were at the motel, we experienced our first swim in the hot springs. New Zealand reminded us of our time in P.N.G. There were sheep walking along paths on the hill, single file. We saw places where there were three-or-four acres of sheep grazing. If we got lost at any time, there was always someone there to give us instructions as to the right way. This happened to us several times during our trip.

In Putaruru, after getting gas and having a cup of coffee, we visited a museum where we got lots of ideas for our Forestry Museum in Powell River. Most of the buildings were closed, as it was early fall in the country. The sawmill and other machinery were on display. We went off on a side road, where we found a rest area to park for the night. In the morning, we went for a walk, then carried on to the town of Waihou, where we purchased some buns and groceries. Our plan was to have breakfast in the Araha, but we were too early, so only got a cup of tea.

At the mining Museum in Waihi, we encountered two interesting things. One was the jail, which had been moved from behind the police station in town, in 1974, and added onto the museum building. The jail had been previously used to hold prisoners in 2 ft. by 4 ft. cells until they could be moved to larger facilities in Hamilton. The jail was a real lock-up, with steel doors that had only a peep-hole and a slot big enough to pass a plate of food. There was a hardwood bed with no mattress. There were not beds in some other cells. Drunks were put in a padded cell, as were violent prisoners. It was not a very pleasant place at all. We learned that, years ago, miners would cut off their thumbs to get compensation. A local doctor had pickled a couple of those thumbs and donated them to the museum when he retired.

We went along a winding road to a 'Hot Water Beach,' but were delayed by some cows on the road. Some cars just plowed through, but we waited for the cows to cross the road. The cows moved slowly in getting out of the way and I was surprised that none got hit. There was no camping on the beach; so we asked a local man where we could stay. He told us "Right through that gate." It was a terrific place. There were hot showers, where we just put a quarter in a slot, turned on the tap and enjoyed a wonderful, warm shower from the hot springs. No more hassle about trying to get the water right. No more hot this moment and cold the next. In the cook kitchen, there was a stove and sink for everyone, tables, toasters, a machine for hot water (boiling) and other necessities. There was also a laundry room with washers and driers. Soap was provided. There were campsites for 115 campers. The campsites were $7 each, which I thought was good.

The next day, we went down to the beach, where we dug a hole in the sand and let it fill up with ocean water. Then we lay in the nice, warm hot-spring water till it got too hot, at which time we got out and waited for the hole to fill up again with cooler ocean water. Some times, we could stay in longer than at other times. It depended on how long it took for the ocean water to come into the hole. If we stayed in too long, we could get burned. There were lots of holes that had been dug in the sand. We also found a cave on this beach, which, of course, we had to explore.

The next few days were spent on the beaches, swimming in the ocean or in hot water pools, and seeing more of the country. We had time to see only part of Northern Island. We noticed how people put their garbage in paper bags, instead of plastic, and their reusable or recyclable refuse was kept separate for pick-up. We also noticed that shoppers get their products in paper bags, or sacks, instead of plastic as we do here.

Our last night. We stayed just outside of Auckland, where, the next day, we returned our mini-van and got the plane for our trip to Australia.

It was a pleasant trip across the Tasman Sea to Australia. In Sydney, we went through customs, got our tickets for the bus to Bandigo, and we were off to see our friend, John Parsons, whom we had met in Lae, P.N.G. when we were there in 1981. John met us at the bus station and took us to a place by a lake where his family was having a picnic. It was for John's mother-in-law's 80th birthday. After a short stay, John drove around town a bit and then took us to his place in Kangaroo Flats. We spent a quiet evening, reminiscing and watching TV. The next day, John took us to a mining museum, where we went on a tour underground. We found it very interesting to learn how they mine gold and got the feeling of what it is like to be 60 metres below ground.

From the mine, we went to see the place where Beryle, John's wife, worked and had lunch with her. We then went to a Tram Museum and took a Tram Tour around the town. In the museum, they had trams of all sizes and ages, some of which are being restored. The trams were from all different places; some were very old. Charlie and I walked around the city centre, where we met John, who took us to a lookout on the mountain, a lumber yard and a couple of other interesting places before going back to his house, where we did some packing, getting ready for the next step of our trip. We phoned our friends, the Staples, to let them know we were coming.

On the way to the airport we stopped to get some mineral water from a tap, then went to a sawmill, where the men took us on a tour of the mill. We found the mill very interesting, because they saved all their short bits of lumber. The men showed us an area in which there had been a bad fire in 1983, in which many people had been killed or injured. All of the houses in the area had been burned to the ground. Thousands of acres of trees had been destroyed. Although the gum and eucalyptus trees had been burned, they did not die and all have been regenerated. But the pines and other trees had to be replanted. Douglas fir, although grown in New Zealand, does not grow in Australia and must be imported from B.C., Washington or Oregon. Some cedar grows in Australia, but most of that has to be imported, too.

At the airport, we said goodbye to our gracious host, John, and boarded our plane for Brisbane, where we were met by Tom Staples, another friend whom we had met in P.N.G. Tom was also a CUSO, but had met and married his wife, Maureen, who was an Australian working in P.N.G. They had come back to Canada to live in Toronto, Tom's home. But Maureen did not like the winters there, so they went back to Australia.

We spent the next few days visiting the Staples and their family, as well as contacting a couple of Charlie's cousins. On one of our many walks, we saw a koala bear in a tree, the first I had ever seen, except in pictures.

Before going to the train station to take the train back to Brisbane, the Staples took us to Bunyan Park, where we got to hold a koala bear and feed a kangaroo. We had to be careful not to hug the bear, as it did not like that and was liable to scratch us. One had to be aware that kangaroos do kick and we could have been hurt by them. One of the boys was kicked by a kangaroo, but not hurt. His father told him that he should have known better than to get behind one.

The train ride through the Australian countryside was very pleasant. At one station, when we stopped, two boys got on the train, waited to see the conductor coming, then got off at the next stop without paying. I guess it was an easy way to get from one station to the next if they had no money.

In Brisbane, after a good night's sleep, we went for a walk over the Story Bridge, had a good breakfast in the Great Wall Café, in a mall, and went back to our hotel to pack for our trip back home. On the bus to Sydney, we saw a motor boat with a man, sitting on a seat, in a parachute which was being towed behind. There were lots of telephones along the highway, and interesting scenery.

Two buns and tea cost $8.50. Wages are less by ½ to ⅓ of what they are here, in B.C., but prices for clothing and food are ½ to double ours. New Zealand and Australia are expensive places to live.

The airline agent informed us that we could only take our luggage to Honolulu. If we had taken the evening flight, we could have gone right through to Vancouver. After much hassle, we caught a different flight to Vancouver. I slept most of the way home. There was a bit of turbulence on take-off, but the rest of the trip was calm.

From Vancouver Airport, we took a bus to the bus station, then went for a walk around Stanley Park. It made me think of the time we had, before we were married, when we visited that park and the zoo and just wandered around.

Except when we were on the ferry, we slept all the way home on the bus. We had been on the go steadily for 56 hours and had jet lag. We got home to Powell River, late and very tired, so went to sleep as soon as our heads hit the pillows.

50 Years Reunion, June 1994 - Grover Cleavland High, Buffalo, New York

Sunday, June 12, 1994: Finish our packing, then catch the 5:30 ferry to Sechelt Peninsula, rest stop in Sechelt, gas-up in Gibsons, catch 8:30 ferry from Langdale and we are on our way for another adventure.

After a brief side trip to see Marty in Squamish, it was back to Vancouver to get the bus tickets we would need for our trip from Toronto back to Vancouver. In order to get the special fare, we had to purchase tickets from Toronto through to Vancouver, even though we would be getting off the bus at Calgary to pick up our van.

After we got the tickets, we were off to Alberta in the van. On the way there were many rest stops, gas-ups and stops to eat; a walk around Kamloops; a motel in Golden; a wait at a construction site; goats on the road; a tour of Field, and we are in Alberta.

Before going to the farm where Krista was, we stopped in Brag Creek to see our friends, Joyce and Gordon, whom we had met some years before at the PNE. Krista and Ralph were working on a cattle ranch near High River. We had a pleasant couple of days with them, helping on the farm and getting to know the area around High River and Okatok. There was a big auction near their place. We went to it and took their sons with us. It was fun looking at all the old machinery and other things on sale. Benjamin bought an old lawn mower, which Charlie and he worked on and got going. While working on the mower, Charlie cut his finger and needed four stitches in it. A day later, as he was looking in the rear of the van, one of the grandsons closed the lid on Charlie's head, cutting it. When we went back to the hospital to get the cut sewed up, one of the nurses advised Charlie to stay away from his grandsons, or be careful of them.

Sunday, June 19 was our 46th wedding anniversary and also Father's Day. After Church, Ralph and Krista drove us to the Calgary Airport to catch our plane to Toronto. We had parked our van at their house for the time we would be gone.

The plane left at 7 p.m. and we were lucky to have a seat near a window.

In Toronto, we took a taxi down to the train station, which we found closed. The taxi driver told us there was an all-night café up the street; so we decided to go there. It was about 2 a.m. and our train left at 9, so we thought the café would be a good place to stay.

As we walked down the street, a couple of cars approached us and the men in them threatened us; so we turned around and went back to the hotel, which was across from the train station. We asked the man behind the desk if we could park on one of the sofas in the lounge till the morning, when we planned to catch a train. He agreed, as long as we did not go to sleep. Well, Charlie did go to sleep on one of the chairs, but I stayed awake and walked around. There were men and women cleaning the lobby, with some vacuuming the rugs, some shining the banisters, etc. Others dusted the tables, lamps and chairs, mopped the tile floors and cleaned the stairs. It was interesting to watch them.

At 5:30 a.m. we went over to the train station, which had just opened, where we walked around and had a little sleep in some of the chairs while we waited to catch our train, which left at 9:00. Charlie and I were so tired that we slept on the train until we were awakened to go through Customs at Niagara Falls. My sister-in-law, Elsie, met us at the Buffalo station when we arrived there at 2 in the afternoon. She told us that my brother Jack was in the hospital and that was why he was not there to meet us. We went to Elsie and Jack's place, where we planned to stay for a few days. We had phoned Elsie from Toronto, so she knew what time we would be in Buffalo.

After we had a bath and a little nap, Elsie took us to Lockport for something to eat. I phoned Krista to let her know that we had arrived safe and sound. That evening we looked at Elsie and Jack's photo albums and talked. We went to bed early, as Charlie and I were tired.

The next day, Tuesday, June 21, after breakfast, Charlie and I went for a walk, talked about old times with Elsie, then went to her daughter's in Lockport for lunch. Nancy showed a video they had made on one of our earlier visits and her son made a video of our present visit. We then went to the hospital in Niagara Falls to see my brother Jack. We had supper in Lewiston, then back to Elsie's, where we talked till late.

In the morning, Wednesday, we just sat around, talked and looked at pictures. I washed my hair and got ready to go out. Elsie needed to go to the bank; so we went to Lockport, where we all had lunch. Charlie had forgotten his camera, so we went back to the house to get it. We then went to Forest Lawn, where my mother was buried. When I saw the stone with her name on it, I collapsed. It was the first time I had seen the stone, as I had left Buffalo before my father purchased it for my mother's grave. We looked at some other stones on graves of our relatives, then left.

After going to visit Elsie's mother in Buffalo, we went with Elsie's sisters, Laura and Helen, to a restaurant for supper. Afterwards, we took Helen home and went with Laura so that she could show us where the bus station was and we could purchase our tickets to Toronto. We took Laura home, then drove along the Niagara River and the Erie Canal on our way back to Elsie's. As we were tired, we just watched a bit of TV and went to bed.

Thursday was our day to start packing and get ready to leave. Charlie and I went for our usual walk. Then we all just sat around, talking. My brother Jack phoned to say good-bye. I told him again how sorry I was that he was in the hospital and hoped he would be better soon. I never saw him again, as he died a few years before I returned to Niagara Falls on our trip across Canada. Elsie gave me my mother's picture that Jack had received from our Granny. As I was the oldest grand-daughter, she felt I should have it.

Friday, June 24, 1944:

Fifty years ago, I graduated from High School. Elsie drove us into Amherst, where our hotel was and where the restaurant of the reunion was. We all went to another restaurant for lunch. Then Elsie left for home. Charlie and I had a rest. Then we got ready to go out. Elsie picked us up and took us to the restaurant where the reunion was. We did not want her to do that, but she insisted. It would not have been a bother to us to get a taxi, and we felt it was an inconvenience for Elsie, though we did appreciate her doing it. The restaurant was not open yet; so we walked around a bit. One thing we noticed was that there was no-one on the street, which we felt was unusual. Later, when we asked Elsie about this, she was upset and said "You do not walk around on the street any more, as there are three-or-more drive-by shootings every day." Many things in Buffalo looked the same, but there were many changes, too. The safety was one thing that had changed, the same as it has everywhere. When we wanted to go back to PNG, a couple of years ago, we received a two-page warning not to go, as there was too much crime there now. It is too bad life has changed in this way.

We had some Chinese tea in a near-by tea shop. Then back to the restaurant, which had opened by then. Many people knew me, but I did not know them. Maybe I did not want to remember, as my High School days were not the happiest for me. It is all behind me now, so I have forgotten it. I am so happy now, and have been for 55 years. I did meet my old Latin teacher, whom I remembered very well. He was a friend of my father's and, if I did not do so well in class, he told my dad. Then I got it from my dad. The teacher was surprised when I told him this. Nobody knew, then, that my dad beat me. I remembered a couple of other teachers who were there. They remembered me, too. My Latin teacher, Mr. Hogan said he was glad I had come, as I was one of his favorite students, even though I was not so good at Latin.

It was funny–I met two girls who had lived near me and whom I had palled around with, but I could not remember anything we did. Strange how I have forgotten so much.

It was a very nice dinner, with a program afterward where they gave gifts to the people who had the most children, the most grandchildren, etc. I won the prize for the one who had come from the farthest away. I got a bottle of wine. Helen and her husband had come from Colorado; so they were anxious to go. We left early with them, as they were staying at a hotel near ours. It was 12:30 when we went to bed.

In the morning, we re-packed our gear in preparation for leaving for home again. Elsie came to the hotel and took us to the bus station. When we got there, we discovered that a bus was just about to leave for Toronto and we decided to take it. The bus driver was kind enough to wait for us while we said good-bye to Elsie, who had gone to park her car.

Going over the Peace Bridge brought many memories from my childhood back to me. In those days, we used to go across the bridge to swim at Fort Erie, as the water was cleaner on the Canadian side. Besides, it was not so developed there. Also, there were no beaches on the Buffalo side, and there were some in Fort Erie. The Peace Bridge was a nice walk for us when we were kids. Sometimes we just went half-way across, but Customs did not like that so much—I do not remember why. The front Park brought back memories to both Charlie and me, as we went there many times when he was in Hamilton and came down to Buffalo on leave. We used to sit on a bench and watch the ships go by on the lake. It was also the place where I told Charlie that I loved him.

In Toronto, we were lucky again and caught an earlier bus to Sudbury. However, we had to wait two hours in Sudbury anyway. There had been a short stop at Fort Erie, but no other stops until we got to Sudbury. It was 7:15 pm when we left Sudbury for Thunder Bay, with stops at Blind River, Sault Ste Marie, Wawa and White River, where we changed drivers. I must have been sleeping, or something, as I did not write any notes as to scenery or anything that we saw or did. Of course, it was dark when we were travelling. Also, there was not much to see, as we were travelling on the big highways or freeways. We arrived in Thunder Bay at 8:05 a.m. and had our breakfast there. Leaving again at 9:30, we had a short stop at Upsala, where I got ice cream and some candy–those were the days when I could have ice cream and candy.

We had 40 minutes at Dryden. My leg was beginning to hurt, as the bus driver would not let me off the bus at some stops where he was delivering, or if he had to wait to let someone off, or someone wanted to get on the bus. This is something I must do–I need to walk around a bit every so often, or my knee will get stiff.

There was a ten-minute rest stop at Kenora, then on to Manitoba, where we went through a place named Reynolds. I wondered if Elsie had relatives there, as her maiden name was Reynolds. We had enough time for supper in Winnipeg, then on to Brandon, Virden, Whitewood and Regina. We had changed busses in Winnipeg and we had another change in Regina, where we found, to our surprise, that we were in Saskatchewan. We left Regina at 1:30 a.m. CST and arrived in Swift Current at 4:20 a.m. on Monday, June 27.

Medicine Hat, 7:15: Breakfast stop, brief stop at a turnout to check tires, and on to Calgary, where we had lunch, phoned Krista, got tickets and took the 3 o'clock bus to High River, Alberta, where Krista met us to take us to her place. Krista and I took Ralph's supper to him where he was working. He did not know that we were coming, so he went home and we missed him. We returned to Krista's, where we talked till late before going to bed.

On Tuesday, we re-packed our bags, did a washing and helped Krista and Ralph around the farm before going to High River to get chicken burgers, which we took out to the place where Ralph was working. Then we went back to town to do some banking and shopping for Krista. Charlie went back out to help Ralph with a machine that he was having trouble with. In the evening, he went back out to help him with the machine again. Krista, her kids and I stayed home to do the farm chores.

On Wednesday, after packing up, we left Krista's and headed west in our Aerostar van, which we had left at her place. We travelled west on the route through Jasper, Golden, Revelstoke, Three-Way Gap, Grimrock, and on down to Kelowna, where we found no-one home at Benita's (our daughter), so travelled on to Summerland. In Penticton, we saw our grandson Orrin. Then on to stop at Yellow Lake, Keremeos, where we stayed behind a fruit stand for the night.

Thursday, June 30, we got up early and had breakfast in Princeton. Then on to Manning Park and Hope, and up the Sea to Sky Highway to see Marty and Meta in Squamish. After supper, Marty's son Skip came with us when we left for Powell River. It was too late to catch a ferry; so we stayed at Portage Cove Campsite for the night.

In the morning, we waited for the campsite gate to be opened, then went down to the ferry landing, where we found a long lineup of cars, etc. We got that ferry, but had to wait at Earl's Cove for the ferry to Saltery Bay.

After taking Skip home, we went home ourselves. It had been a good trip and we had enjoyed it.

B.C. Rail Cariboo Prospector September 1998

Thursday, September 24: After final packing and doing other necessary business and visits, we left on the 11:30 ferry from Saltery Bay. We stopped in Sechelt; so just made the ferry from Langdale. As we planned to be at the Cawfield Shopping Center in the spring to operate a children's workshop, we decided to stop to see the manager about our plans.

At the B.C. Rail train station in North Vancouver, we got our tickets and parked the van in the place where we intended to leave it. We walked around the area, had some supper and returned to the station, where we did some reading, watched the activities around the station and just relaxed. We slept that night in our van in the parking lot, as our train did not leave till 7 in the morning. It was a noisy night, with lots of traffic on the street, but we managed to get some sleep.

It was an early start for us in the morning. The train was right on time and we were on our way without any delays. All meals were served on the train.

En route, we went through the rail yards of North Vancouver, where there were lots of freight cars and engines. Up Howe Sound, past Brandywine Falls, past other falls with a stop at Whistler, where skiers and others detrained. Onward, following the Gold Rush Trail through the Bridge River area, 100 Mile House, Williams Lake and Quesnel. Besides the beautiful falls, the lakes and forest, we went across some deep canyons. One that impressed everyone was a very deep canyon over the Fraser River, where the train stopped in the middle of the bridge to let people enjoy the view. It was a bit scary, though. Some places along the way were beside steep rock or through rock tunnels in the mountain.

I am not sure where, but the train also made a stop beside a huge waterfall, which was a spectacular view. The only wildlife I have noted was a mountain goat that we saw somewhere on the route.

The meals on the train were fabulous, served by a courteous and helpful staff.

Except for Whistler, the train made only one stop, which was at Lillooet, for about ten minutes, before arriving at Prince George. This was the end of our train trip. Some people took another train to Prince Rupert, while others got a train to Banff or Jasper. It had been a pleasant, enjoyable trip, and we were glad we had chosen the train.

In Prince George, we attended the AGM of Canadian Women in Timber. After the meeting, our son Marty met us and we went to his place for a few days. Shortly after we left Prince George we discovered we had not turned in our hotel key—Charlie thought I had done it and I thought he had. So, back to the hotel to take the key back. Then we stopped at a McDonalds just outside of town, where we each had a hamburger. Then we were on our way with no further delays.

Moose can be a problem on the roads up north. There have been several accidents where people hit moose crossing the road. There were signs on the side of the highway, warning people of the danger. As we passed one of these signs, showing a picture of a moose, my always-joking granddaughter shouted "Moose!" Marty stepped on the brake. "Where? Where?" he asked. "On the sign," was her reply.

During our stay in MacKenzie, Marty took us fishing, then for a ride up the mountain, and showed us a wonderful time. He had taken a few days off so he could be with us. We were able to see our niece and her family, a friend that had moved to MacKenzie, and another friend that we had met when we demonstrated our sawmill at his school a few years before.

After a pleasant visit with Marty and our granddaughter Martina, we got the bus to go home again. The ride to Prince George was comfortable, but we did not see much, as it was dark. There was a one-hour wait at the Prince George bus station, where we had to change busses. On the way south, there were stops at Williams Lake, Quesnel, 100 Mile House, Cache Creek, Hope and a couple of other small places. That bus ride was the worst Charlie and I had ever experienced. Even though I am only 4 feet 9 inches tall, my knees bumped into the back of the seat in front of us. That is how close the seats were. I felt sorry for people who were taller, especially a man over 6 feet.

At the Vancouver bus station, we got a taxi to the B.C. Rail train station, where we picked up our van and headed home again. It was midnight, September 30.

The train trip was wonderful, and I would recommend it to everyone, but I sure would not advise anyone to take the bus trip from Prince George to Vancouver, unless the company changes the seating.

The Royal Hudson - June 1991

We had gone to Penticton to attend our grandson Orrin's graduation from high school. It had been a pleasant visit with our daughter Krista and her family, during which, we visited the Game Farm, where there were different animals in as close to their natural settings as was possible. The Game Farm was divided into large areas where buffalo, lions and other animals were kept in natural environments. Snakes and the like were kept in cages in a separate building, as were the birds. We also went on several picnics, on walks, just relaxed and enjoyed having fun with our grandchildren. We had brought our small double bike; so we went on bike rides too. Charlie had taken a small bike and put an extra seat between the handle bars and his seat for me to sit on. It fit just nicely on a bracket at the back of our Aerostar.

After this visit, we went to Kelowna to visit our other daughter and her family. Benita was working; so we took our grandson Scott everywhere with us, when we went shopping, on walks, or on hikes up the mountain. On one shopping trip, we came upon an advertisement for a trip on the Royal Hudson Steam Train. We decided to stop in North Vancouver on our way home and take this trip. There was a travel stand near by, so we reserved our seats. We paid for our tickets when we got to the North Vancouver train station. As the train did not leave til the next morning, we stayed that night in a trailer park under the Lions Gate Bridge. To spend our time, while waiting, we went for bike rides around the site. We did not go out on the street, as there was too much traffic. When the traffic on the bridge had calmed down a bit, we went for a walk across and back. From the bridge, we could see the boats and trains moving below, as well as people walking on the sea wall. The next day, we were up early to catch the train. It was a lovely sunny day, which added to the pleasure of our trip.

June 19, 1991, our 43rd Wedding Anniversary:

Engine #32869-B.C.'s Queen of the Rails. It was the train that carried King George and Queen Elizabeth on part of their continent-wide tour in 1939. Now it was carrying us. It was the black beauty of early Canadiana. As we travelled, the train hugged the rough shore of Howe Sound from North Vancouver to Squamish. It made a brief stop at Brittania Beach to let people off who wished to go to the B.C. Museum of Mining. From there, they could take a bus to Squamish, where they could get the train, or a boat, back to North Vancouver. They could also take another train and travel north to Prince George.

The scenery was wonderful on the train trip to Squamish. It was interesting to see the cars going along on the highway above us and to note the boats below, or sometimes beside us.

After a couple of hours in Squamish, where we walked around town and had something to eat, we returned to the station and boarded the boat which was docked just the other side of the tracks. It was a pleasant sea trip on the quiet waters of Howe Sound. As I seem to be one who does not write down too much in her notes of what she sees, I cannot remember exactly what I did see, but I know I enjoyed it.

As the boat docked in Vancouver, we had to take a taxi back to the North Vancouver train station, where we picked up our car and made a wild dash to Horseshoe Bay to catch the ferry for home.

China 1988

We had met Bernie Harris and her husband at the Junior Forest Wardens' National Campout in Oyama the August before. She was there with her husband, John, who was one of the instructors at the camp. We were there with our sawmill, demonstrating its operation. The wardens were helping us on the mill and were building small wood products. There was a shortage of tables. So they cut the lumber and some of the parents of the wardens, with the wardens' help, built some more. Charlie showed the wardens how to make stilts; they all wanted to make a pair. Everywhere we went in the camp, we could see someone on stilts. On the last day of the camp, the staff organized a stilt race, which was lots of fun, for wardens and spectators.

Bernie and her husband became good friends of ours and we visited them several times at their home in Victoria. On a trip in January of 1988, while we were visiting them, Bernie mentioned that she and some other teachers planned to take some of their students to China during the spring break. She asked us if we would be interested in joining them. We thought that would be a good idea, as Charlie had always wanted to go to China. Over the next couple of months, we made two more trips to Victoria and plans were made for the trip in March.

On March 27, 1988 we left Powell River in a 170 Cessna (small plane) for Vancouver, where we would meet the group from Victoria. While waiting for the 1:45 plane to China, we walked around the terminal with the group, looking in all the shops.

On the flight, we were given peanuts, drinks and lunch, as well as apples and oranges. It was nice to be able to walk around on the plane. We did not see much out of the windows, as we were flying above the clouds. There were five movies shown on a big screen; two were in English and the others were in Chinese. After supper, we were asked to fill out some papers for the Customs. Somehow, I had difficulty filling them out. As a matter of fact, mine were a real mixed-up mess. First, there was no carbon; so I did not make a second copy. On the second try, somehow, I got smudges all over the paper. With the third try, I finally got it right.

Monday, April 28, 7 p.m., Shanghai Airport:

Go through Customs (no problems), meet our guide, take a bus to our hotel, check into our room and have another supper. Our room, as in the other hotels we stayed in, was very comfortable, with all the luxuries we needed, including hot water in jugs for washing our faces and cleaning our teeth, as well as fresh cold water to drink. We were advised not to use the tap water for drinking or brushing our teeth.

Even though it was nighttime, Charlie and I went for a walk along the street. We had nothing to fear. The people we met all gave us a friendly smile and greeting. We both had a good night's sleep after a warm bath. I must have gotten hungry, because I wrote in my notes, "ate orange at 3 a.m."

The next day, Charlie and I got up early and went for a walk before breakfast, which, like all of the meals we had, was big, with lots of variety. I had a cup of tea, which was black, and discovered that the Chinese do not know how to make Western tea. I think they must boil it, or something, because it was so strong, and no amount of sugar could change the taste. From then on, I ordered green tea only. After this, as we travelled, somehow the waiters seemed to know my preference, as they served me green tea without my asking.

This was our first day in China. It was filled with lots of activity, just like the days that followed. There was always a big bus to take us around. We were amazed at the development that we saw. There seemed to be all the modern conveniences that we have in Canada. There was a mixture of traffic, from large trucks and busses to smaller trucks and busses, cars, bicycles, rickshaws, carts, and people walking. The city streets were so wide: There were four lanes on each side, with a wide sidewalk for people and two lanes for bicycles, then another four lanes for motor vehicles in the centre. It was crowded, but we were told that there were very few accidents. Everyone seemed so patient and courteous. Another thing that amazed us were the traffic lights. There were dials beside the lights which told the drivers how many minutes or seconds before the light would change. This meant we knew exactly when the light would turn from red to green, or the reverse. No one ever jumped the light. We noticed a couple of traffic policemen, but not many.

On our first day, we were taken to a commune, where we were given tea, as was the custom. The people were very friendly. Through an interpreter, we were able to ask them questions and inquire about their life in China.

From there, we went to a pearl factory to see the beautiful work the people do with pearls. Then we visited a playschool, where the children of the workers are well looked after while their parents work.

In China, everyone who is capable works. Others, who are not capable, are looked after by their families, or are in homes. Some older people look after younger members of the family. We learned, from one grandmother, that she felt it was a mistake to allow only one child to a woman. She felt it spoiled the one child. The women should be allowed two children, so that one child does not get everything. We were free to walk around the area near the playschool. Then we had lunch at a local restaurant.

The bus driver took us for a ride around the town and stopped to let some of the people take pictures of a brick factory. Then it was off to a carpet factory, where we watched people work. We were given time to buy gifts if we wanted to. One lady bought a beautiful rug, to be sent home. Many bought gifts when we went to the big shopping mall known as the Shanghai Independent Exhibition Hall. From the top floor of the building, people were able to get pictures of the city.

The Children's Palace was next on our agenda. It was a wonderful place, where the children gave a short musical concert. Several times on our trip, children sang to us. Everywhere we went, they sang the song *Red River Valley*. It was the only Canadian song that they knew, I guess. It was always so beautiful. The children showed us the art work they had done, or were doing. Many other artistic talents, such as literature, are learned in the centre.

After another ride around the city and supper at another restaurant, we returned to our hotel, the Yen Feng Guest House. As Charlie and I were very tired, we went to bed early.

As was our usual custom, we were up early and went for a walk before breakfast. We needed to do this to get an appetite for the big meals they served. This day, the bus took us to the white jade factory and temple where, as in all the other factories we visited, we saw the excellent work the people were doing. The people we saw in China were very skilled and did beautiful work.

From the jade factory, we went to the beautiful Shonhae Gardens, where we were free to walk among the many gorgeous flowers, trees and plants. We all admired the stone figures and fountains. One thing we noticed there was that rocks were piled on top of one another to form beautiful art. The people of China are very artistic.

Lunch was at another hotel. Then the group was free to go shopping or just walk around. It was so nice, the way we were getting to see the city. Charlie and I, with some of the others, went down to the harbor, where we walked around and talked to the people; many of them could speak English well.

The group then went for a river cruise, where we watched a magician's show on the boat. The bus then took us to the Palace Hotel for supper, after which we were taken to a circus show. The performances were marvellous, especially the bear acts and the trapeze act. On the way back, we noticed lots of boats on the river. Charlie and I again went to bed shortly after we returned to the hotel.

Thursday, our third day in China:

We packed our bags, had breakfast and left on the bus for the train station. There, we walked around, did some shopping and waited for the train to Suzhow, which was Victoria BC's twin city. Many communities or organizations in Canada have twin cities in other countries where they share ideas and knowledge of their different ways of life with each other.

After checking into the hotel in Suzhow, we had lunch. It was served in the same way as all of our other meals: We sat around a large table with a raised portion in the middle that rotated with bowls of various foods on it. There were usually from five to eight different dishes. Then, when we thought we could not eat any more, they came up with big bowls of soup and various desserts. Of course, there was plenty of tea and coffee.

After lunch the bus took us to see Tiger Hall, where we climbed six or seven flights of stairs to the pagoda. This, like all the places we went to, was very interesting and worth the climb. From the top of the pagoda we could see all around the area. The bus then took us to the Lingering Gardens, with their many works of art and sculpture.

Next on the agenda was the Silk Institute and Embroidery Store, where we were given a fashion show of the wonderful gowns, etc. made in the institution. There was what was known as the Friendship Store, where one was free to buy the many beautiful things on display.

We then walked around another place, called the Free Market, where people displayed their produce. This was similar to what we call a flea market in Canada, or the Farmers' Market in Powell River. After supper in a place nearby, we again went through the market, then back to the Soochow Hotel. Charlie and I took a walk in the moonlight around the hotel gardens. It was beautiful to see the moon shining through a moon gate. It was an experience we will never forget. Moon gates are round stone structures which are traditional in China.

After breakfast, the next day, the bus took us to visit some gardens, another silk factory and store, a wool factory with a fashion show and a store, and to the garden of Hon. Administrator. At each place we visited in China, we were served with tea and goodies. We had lunch, that day, by a big lake and the Grand Canal. I believe this was the place where we saw a large, exquisite stone houseboat that a man had made for his daughter. I am not sure of the story behind it all.

After lunch, it was another afternoon of activity. We went to a fan factory. I bought a beautiful fan and a wall hanging. We also went to the North Temple Pagoda, with its beautiful statues of Buddha. Buddha statues are in all of the temples and in different places, as Buddhism is the religion of the Chinese. The people are very devoted to their religion.

Before supper, we went to a jade factory where, as in other factories, there was a shop where we could buy the products made in the factory.

The bus took us to supper, then to the Palace Theatre, where we listened to the Suswap Band in concert. That was where we met the Mayor of Suzhow. I am not sure where it was, but we did get to see the plaque sent to Suzhow by Victoria BC. Many of the people in our group were tired and went to bed as soon as we got back to our hotel.

Saturday:

We again packed our bags and went back down to the train station. After a short walk around the area, we boarded the train for Chanzhow. Whether we were put in a special place on the train, I do not know, but where we were, the seats were very comfortable. From the window, we could see the many greenhouses and gardens along the tracks, as well as in the fields. Unfortunately, there were also plastic and styrofoam cups and containers that had been thrown from the train.

We got settled in our hotel rooms in Chanzhow, had lunch and an hour-and-a-half nap, then went to a school where one of the Victoria high school teachers was from.

Central High in Victoria was the school the teachers and students with us attended. We met many of the students at the Chanzhow School. After that visit, we went back to the hotel for supper and a free evening, which I am sure many of the group appreciated. Charlie and I went for a short walk, just to relax.

Sunday:

It was hard to believe, but a week had gone by since we had come to China. After breakfast at our hotel, we visited a comb factory, where I was talked into purchasing a special comb that would be good for my long hair. The man who was demonstrating the combs gave the women (and the men) advice on "care of your hair."

The bus then took us to a housing project, where we saw apartments and gardens which, as usual, were very beautiful. The apartments were small, but neat and adequate. People may say that the guides took us only to places that they wanted us to see, but Charlie and I were free to go wherever we wanted. On the first evening that we were in China, we had taken a walk around Shanghai. There, as on other walks that we took, we met lots of people, visited places that were not on the agenda and some of the homes. No-one ever said anything or attempted to stop us. The people we met were well-dressed and looked happy. They appeared to be well looked after.

Before lunch, on our second Sunday, we went to the Buddha Temple and the Garden of Heavenly Tranquil. China has many gardens that the people can enjoy. They are all so beautiful and are always full of people.

Back at the hotel, we packed up, had lunch and waited for the bus to take us on a trip down to the canal. Here, we saw men carrying bricks, in bamboo baskets on their shoulders, from the boat to the shore. There are a lot of people in China and, to keep them employed, some things are done the hard way. There is also very technical development happening. During our stay at the canal, we were able to walk around and went to a fabric factory, where we saw the machines operating in the mill. In this factory, the design is printed on the fabric by a machine. In the other factories that we visited, like the silk factory, the design is embroidered by hand.

After a walk around the town centre, we went to another Children's Palace, where we heard a concert on traditional Chinese instruments. We were able to talk to the music students, who showed us their instruments and how they worked. They then gave our group a chance to try to play any that they wished to. I don't think any of us did very well on our tries. We then went back to the hotel for supper and a rest in the meeting room, as we had left our rooms that morning. The bus then took our group to the railroad station to catch the train for Nanjing. It was a little late picking us up, and we almost missed the train. We were crowded into sleeping compartments. Although there was an upper and a lower bunk, Charlie and I only used the lower bunk. When we got to Nanjing, the group was settled into the Hotel of Lotus flowers.

Monday, April 4:

The beginning of our last week in China. After we took a walk and had our breakfast, the bus took us to Su Jen Mausoleum, where we had 39 sets of two steps up to the Chiang Kaishek Garden Monastery, which was a building made of bricks. We then went to the Tomb of the Emperor, with an animal road, which was very interesting. On each side of the road were statues of animals made of stone. There were animals like elephants, camels, lions, etc. Between them were decorative trees or shrubs. We visited other roads, but I only recall this one. Some things have stuck in my mind, but, as I did not write them down, I am not sure where they were. However, I do believe the tomb of the Emperor was the place where we went underground to see a casket on a raised bench in the middle of a room. Then we went down a long, narrow hall to view different Chinese treasures in glass cases. I remember that it was hot and dark in there.

After a drive around the area to view the gardens, cemetery and such, we returned to our hotel for lunch. Then we went on a cruise along the Yang-tze-kiang. We all found this very enjoyable and interesting, as we got to see some of the activity on the river as well as on the shoreline. Some of the people in the group did not go on the cruise, so we went back to the hotel afterward. I believe it was on that cruise that we saw a bridge that is famous in China. Unfortunately, the story behind the building of it has slipped my mind, for I am sure it was a good story.

After picking up the few who did not go on the cruise, the bus took us to the Jade Gardens, where all the statues were made of either black or green jade. As usual, it was all so beautiful and interesting. There was a store there, too, where one could buy figurines made of jade.

The city wall and a shopping centre were next on our list. At the centre, we walked around and had a drink (some people had two or three) of Chinese wine or liquor. The bus then took us to a park, where we walked around the beautiful lake and back to our hotel for supper. It was a very pleasant walk.

Some of the group found the distance too great and took the bus back. Others, like Charlie and I, found the walk more enjoyable, as the weather was so gorgeous. After supper, Charlie and I went for another walk before taking a bath and going to bed early. The luxurious warm baths in the evening were something we really enjoyed. The group always stayed in the best hotels with all the amenities.

Tuesday morning was the same: pack up, have breakfast and go for a walk while we waited for the bus to take us to the airport, where we caught the plane for Beijing (former Peking).

From the airport in Beijing, we went to the Temple of Heaven and then had lunch. We learned that many people belonged to 2-bike families, like we have 2-car families. There were parking areas of three levels, where people parked their bikes. It was a strange thing to see. It was just like our parking areas in Vancouver, except that there were bikes there instead of cars. Most people travel to work on bikes. We saw hundreds of them travelling down the busy streets. The bus often took the back roads to avoid the bikes and other traffic.

Before lunch, we walked around the square where the restaurant was. The stores were decorated in many colors and designs. After lunch, the bus took us to our hotel, where the room assigned to Charlie and me had a leaky bathroom. The manager quickly gave us another room. That evening, we were free to do as we chose.

In the morning of the next day, we went to the Mao Mausoleum. There were lots of people lined up to go into the building, but, when the group came, we were taken ahead of all of them. I found this a bit embarrassing. Mao was in a glass casket in the centre of a well-lit room. The guide told us that it really was the body of Mao, and not a made-up duplicate. The building containing Mao was in the famous Tiananmen Square. The Imperial Palace and the Forbidden City are also in the Square. We were given the opportunity to visit these buildings too. Tiananmen Square is an interesting place, where many people came, as it was a great place to fly your kite. Charlie bought three kites from the vendors who were in the Square, but he has yet to fly any of them.

After the usual wonderful lunch, the bus took us to the Summer Palace, which was on a beautiful lake. This was where the stone boat was. It sat on the side of the lake. The man who built it never used it. Why he built it, I am not sure, but it was sure big. The Winter Palace was also on this lake. I think this was where we went through the bridgeway that ran along beside the lake, where there were beautiful flowers planted in boxes. We then went to another factory and to a zoo, where, for the first time, I saw a panda bear. Panda bears are famous in China and very much prized.

That night, we had the famous Peking Duck supper, with wine and all the trimmings. We were all really stuffed and were glad to get back to the hotel, where we could have a hot bath and go to bed. We noted, that day, the big cars with the curtains drawn on the windows. We were told they were the cars used to carry the diplomats.

Time was sure going fast. We only had three more days in China. The next day, we went to the Ming Tombs, stopping to shop at a free market on the way. We also had time to walk around the area, where there were more stone statues of animals. We saw a line of live camels, and some of our group had rides on one, but Charlie would not let me go.

We then went to the Great Wall of China and climbed it, after having lunch at a local café. It was a strenuous climb, but well worth it, even if it was only to say "I climbed the Great Wall of China." A man, who was much older than I was, helped me up one place where it was extra steep. We could climb up to a level spot, where there was a tower, and see all over the countryside. The wall is continually up and down for miles, going from one tower to the next. We have heard of some people who have walked the full length of it. One or two have done it on bikes. We only did the walk to one tower and back down again. It was much easier coming down.

According to Luo Zhewen, in the book *The Great Wall,* the Great Wall crosses the vast area from the Yalu River to the Qilianshan and Tianshan mountains and across pasturelands and deserts. It has a long history of over twenty dynasties and feudal principalities in the last 2000 years.

Astronauts, looking back from space, have said the Great Wall was the most conspicuous of all man-made projects. It is one of the wonders of the world and is the pride of China. The Great Wall was built and rebuilt in strategic places as a defence for China. Over the years it has proven to be an excellent defence. With its nine borders and eleven fortressed towns, it totals 70,000 kilometres or longer and was manned by a force of over nine million. It was built by the hard labor and wisdom of the Chinese people. It was a tremendous task of construction, when you consider the difficulties of mountains, gullies, deserts, and pastureland which was crossed without the aid of modern transport.

Legend has reported that the bricks, mortar and stones were carried on the backs of men. The work was done along narrow pathways, where the men stood in line and passed the materials from one hand to another. This avoided people bumping into one another and raised efficiency. Hand carts, rolling logs, etc. were also used. On mountain tops, windlasses were installed to hoist the huge stones. Mortar, bricks and the like were transported by cableways, which were made by fixing cables on the two sides of a valley or gully. Sheep and donkeys were also used, as they were good mountain climbers. It can be said that the Great Wall was built by the hard labour of the Chinese people.

We purchased the above-mentioned book when we were in China. It is an excellent story of the Great Wall with very good descriptions and many pictures. The story and the captions under the pictures are in both English and Chinese.

Now, to continue with the story of our trip: After the Great

Wall, the bus took us back to town for supper and then we went to the opera. Some of the group enjoyed it very much (very few), but others, like Charlie and I, did not understand it. During the intermission, the guide asked us if we wanted to go. He told those who wanted to stay for the second half of the opera that the bus would come back later to get them.

Charlie and I had a TV in our room. So, when we got back to the hotel, we watched the TV, which had an English channel.

On Friday, when we were again packing, we found we had bought too much to get into our suitcases. So, later, when we went to Friendship Store, we bought a new suitcase. It was a neat brown bag that had wheels on the bottom and a zipper near the bottom that, when opened, expanded into a larger bag. The Friendship Store was a large department store exclusively for foreign visitors. When we entered China, we had to exchange our money for currency that was made especially for foreigners. There was a fine for people of China who kept any of this money. If they received any, they must exchange it as soon as possible.

The only problem we had in China was that Charlie and I, and some of the others, got sore throats. But they did not last long.

After lunch and shopping, we went to the train station for our trip to Tianjen. In Tianjen it was a struggle to carry our gear from the train station to the bus when we got there. It was the first time that there was no one to carry our bags. At the other places, there was always someone assigned to help us. We went shopping in the Free Market and then in the Mall, where we had supper. After that, we were taken to check into our hotel. As we were all very tired, we went to bed early.

In the morning, we re-packed our bags so that they would be easier to carry. For the first time, we were late in going to breakfast, but no one seemed to notice. However, we did have to eat in a hurry, as the bus was already there, waiting for the group. We went to a jade and ivory factory to see the skilled workers and the wonderful work they do. Then we went to the Painting Institute and saw the beautiful paintings done by hand. Before going back to the hotel for lunch, we went to a book store and another Friendship Store.

After lunch, we went to a Middle School. There, we met many of the students. One of the girls we met became our pen pal and wrote to us for several years. Another girl told us that they wanted to listen to us speak, because their teacher was Australian and had an accent. She said we spoke better English.

Before going back to the hotel for a rest and supper, we went to a Museum of Natural Science.

As it was our last night in China, and we had to get up early to get the train back to Beijing, we did our final packing and went to bed early.

Sunday, April 10:
Our last day in China and the day of our trip home. We were up at 3:45 a.m. We packed our things, making sure we had everything. Then we were off on the bus to the train station. We again had to carry our own bags. There was a short wait for the train. Breakfast was on the train, in a separate dining room from the rest of the passengers.

From the train station in Beijing, we went to the airport. From there, we went to a square, where the group was allowed to shop, walk around or do whatever they pleased for two hours before we went to lunch.

Back at the airport, we were told to go to the International Terminal, where we caught the 2 p.m. plane. We had been waiting since 11:30, since the plane was late. The plane went to Shanghai first, where we all went through Customs. We then walked around, did more shopping and just relaxed. The plane was called. People went down the ramp, but the plane was not there. So we had to wait until 4 p.m., when we were finally off to Vancouver BC.

After going through Customs in Vancouver, we got our tickets to Powell River and home. Our plane did not leave for a couple of hours. So we had a cup of tea and a do-nut. (I could have my favorite treat, a do-nut, at that time.) We then sat around the airport and relaxed. Charlie slept a bit.

POWELL RIVER BC:
Home again. We took a taxi from the airport to our house, had a glass of wine to celebrate our trip, then a cup of tea. As we were tired, or had jet-lag, or it was the wine, we both fell asleep on the sofa.

When I woke up, I did not know where I was, for a while. Then I realized we were home again.

It was an excellent experience. We learned a lot and had a lot of fun. A trip to China is a trip everyone who can should make. They will enjoy it, like Charlie and I did.

Princess Auto Inventors Fair - June 1999 & 2000
Winnipeg, Manitoba

Our first invite to the Princess Auto Inventors Fair came in 1997. We had been customers of Princess Auto for many years, since first ordering parts for our excavating equipment back in the 1960s. It was a mail-order company in Winnipeg then. At the time, they sold used and new military equipment as well as other new parts.

In about 1974 we had stopped in Winnipeg on our way home from Kingston, where we had visited my grandmother. Princess Auto was mostly a warehouse, then. It was an amazing place. There were shelves and shelves of old dusty parts, motors, and everything imaginable. Charlie and I spent several hours there, just looking, before going back to catch our train again. We had detrained the night before and had gone into a hotel for the night.

Before catching our train after our visit to Princess Auto, we went to the Museum of Natural Science, which was near our hotel. It was also near the train station. The museum was a wonderful place with two or three floors of exhibits of nature, wildlife and the environment. We were unable to go to the Fair in 1997 because Charlie had had an accident with the truck and it had not been repaired at that time. In 1998, we again had to put off our trip to Winnipeg, because Charlie was in the hospital after having an operation on his neck.

June 1999:

We are again planning to go. Final preparation done on June 2 and we were off, on the 7:30 ferry from Saltery Bay, with our camper and all of our gear on the truck. We gassed up at Gibsons and stayed the night in the Langdale ferry landing so that we could get an early start on Thursday. Breakfast on the ferry, gas up again in Chilliwack, and we are on our way on Highway 101 to Hope with no problems. Steam pours out of the radiator as we climb the steep hills just before the Hope Slide. We stop at the slide to let the truck cool off, then go a little further, when the rad heats up again. We cool off the truck again, then return to Hope. The radiator heats up again, but with lots of water we are able to keep it from boiling.

We thought about renting a U-Haul, but changed our minds when we considered leaving the truck somewhere. After much discussion, we decided to take the truck home and go to Winnipeg some other way. We caught the 7:25 ferry from Horseshoe Bay and arrived home at midnight.

On Tuesday, June 8, we were off for Winnipeg again, this time by bus. We discovered we could have gone by train cheaper, as there was a deal on by which two seniors could travel for the price of one. We had packed our photo albums, that showed what we do and what inventions we had intended to bring if we had come in the truck. We also had a few of our smaller inventions, like the wooden cookies.

The bus to Winnipeg did not leave until much later, so we had time to browse around the station. The move of the bus station into the same building as the train station was a very good idea, as it made things so much easier for people who had to travel to Vancouver by bus and then take a train, or the reverse. This proved very good when we travelled across Canada by train a few years later. Another thing that was good was that there was so much more to do if you had to wait for a bus or train. While we waited, we walked in a nearby park, looked into the shops in the station, sat in the restaurant and just relaxed on the station seats. There seemed to be lots to read around the station.

The bus trip was interesting, but you could not walk around on the bus like you could on a train. Our bus must not have been an express bus, as we made lots of stops on the way. If there was a 10-minute or more stop, we could get off to walk around. Less than 10 minutes, and you had to stay on the bus, although the driver did let people off if they were desperate for a smoke while he loaded passengers or freight.

Our first long stop was 30 minutes at Kamloops for a quick

breakfast. Lunch was in Calgary, where we changed busses and had time to walk around. A 30-minute stop and supper in Medicine Hat, then on to Saskatchewan. Each time we entered a new province, we had to change the time on our watches. At Gull Lake, we nearly left a young girl behind. She had gone off the bus to have a smoke, or something, and the driver had not known she had got off. We had been told never to leave the bus unless the driver said it was OK. He told us there were two toilets at the rear of the bus if we needed them. When the bus began to move without the girl, some of the passengers told the driver and he waited for her. He was not happy about it, though. A 40-minute stop in Swift Current for a cup of tea, then a sleep till we got to Moose Jaw.

It was now June 10. There was another change of busses in Regina and, before we knew it, we were in Brandon, Manitoba for breakfast. From Brandon, we had an express bus with no stops till we were in Winnipeg. Dan, from Princess Auto, met us at the bus station and, after picking up some people at the airport, took us to our hotel. We checked in, got settled and had a rest. Later, Dan picked us up and took us to Princess Auto, where we established where we would be for the fair.

After getting back to the hotel, Charlie and I went for a walk to a local Safeway, where we got some milk and donuts and had an ice cream cone. (Those were the good old days when I could have a donut and an ice cream cone—before this diabetic thing.) We watched TV and retired for a good night's sleep.

Friday, June 11:

Our first day on the site. We set up our table and met the other inventors. Two of them, Dave Tucker from England and his friend Murray from Ontario became good friends of ours. They were in the same hotel as we were, so we seemed to pal around with them when we were at the fair.

At the Inventor's Fair there were lots of backyard inventions. It was good that people had a chance to share and exchange their ideas. They got help from each other on how to improve their own inventions and gave others advice on theirs. Two women, who were also in our hotel, had invented a sock that fit over a phone receiver to prevent one from getting germs, etc. when using a pay phone or other strange phone. Dave had invented a type of special plastic for picture frames or display frames. Murray had devised a method of separating two children in a bed. It consisted of a soft roll that you put in between the children. This would work well if the children were of different sexes.

Another man, Ken Nolman, had improved his 0.9 metre-high remote control payloader, which can operate for an hour and 45 minutes on a litre of gas. The kids—of all ages—at the fair enjoyed watching it work. The new version of the machine runs on gas and can lift 127 kilograms. Ken built the loader to clear his sidewalk of the Winnipeg snow. One of the rules at the fair was no selling, so he could not put his machine on sale until after the show.

There was a man who invented a way to heat his motorcycle handlebars with the engine jacket water. Another man invented a machine that measures the speed of your slap-shot. A farmer, who seemed to be spending a lot of time on his tractor moving a hay baler eight kilometres to his pasture, invented a 'bale buggy' that can either be mounted or pulled by a truck and can hold and unroll two bales of hay. He estimated this device saved him $5000 in fuel and he had to bring his cattle in for only six weeks the year before.

At this fair, or the one a little later in 2000, there was a fellow who had a device, or crane, on the back of his pickup that allowed him to lift things onto his truck. There was also a sawmill at one of the fairs that was entirely automatic—you just dialed the numbers and the mill cut out the lumber sizes you wanted.

At the '99 fair, since we were limited to what we could carry with us, Charlie and I had a small picture display of his wheelchairs and forestry inventions, such as his log transporters.

There were other inventions at the fair, but I cannot remember the details of them now, as I failed to write them down in my notes. We had a good time comparing notes and ideas with the many new people we met.

While on our daily walk one afternoon, we decided to take the train, instead of the bus, back to Vancouver. One of the staff took me to the train station to get our tickets. When we were in the train-bus station in Vancouver, on our way to the fair, the agent at the wicket had showed me the advertisement in the train magazine with the coupon for the two-for-one fare. I had assumed the Winnipeg station would have the same offer in their magazine. Well, I was wrong, and I had not brought the one I had picked up in Vancouver with me to the Winnipeg station. The driver had to take me back to the hotel to get it. We returned to the station and I got our tickets with no problem. Then we went back to the fair.

Saturday was our second day at the fair, where we met more people and had more fun. Lunch was provided by the staff, as it had been on Friday. That night there was a dinner and dance. Prizes were given out for the best inventions in each category. Charlie and I got a $300 prize as the most innovative inventors. We also were given $300 from the other inventors to help us with our expenses. As usual, I was out on the floor, dancing with the others and having lots of fun. One time, there were eight or more women dancing in a circle. Funny how I can remember that dance so clearly, but cannot remember the inventions that were at the fair.

Sunday, our day to leave. Dan, from Princess Auto staff, came to our hotel and drove Charlie, me and the girls who were with us in the hotel down to the train station. He then took the girls downtown to go shopping. Dave and Murray went to the place where they had parked Murray's pickup. They then left for Ontario.

As our train was not to leave until 6 p.m. and Dan had brought us to the station at 11 a.m., Charlie and I had lots of time to spare. We put our luggage in a locker and went for a walk around the station area. There was a market close by that had once been a train roundhouse. We spent a couple of hours there. It was an amazing place, in a large building with every kind of store you could imagine, from fruit stands and grocery stores to clothing stores, craft shops and souvenir shops. It was like a small Edmonton Mall. There were a couple of parks nearby too, and we walked all around them. We explored a couple of other buildings too. In one of the parks, some musicians were playing. When they were through, another group did some acting.

The train was over two hours late. So we had a nice rest while we waited. We did not leave till 8:35.

On our way back to Vancouver, we had short stops at Portage La Prairie, North Brampton and several other places. Charlie and I slept most of the way. This is one thing that is good about travel by train—you can sleep in the spacious, comfortable seats, and you can walk around. Another thing is having the toilets with a sink and mirror as well.

It was 4:20 a.m. when we found ourselves in Saskatoon, Sask. where we had to wait for a couple of freight trains to pass. We liked to go to the dome car, where we could see where we were going and all the scenery around.

Alberta:
A twenty-minute stop in Edmonton, where we were able to walk around. At Evansburg, we stayed on the train for lunch. Although some people did get off, we felt there was not enough time to go into the station for lunch.

A thirty-minute stop in Jasper, where, to our surprise, it was hot, but we went for a walk around the station area anyhow.

It was so beautiful, going through the mountains. It made us appreciate B.C. and nature. On the way through the interior and down the Fraser Canyon, we slept all the way. From Mission to Vancouver, we travelled on the CP line, as men were working on the CN tracks. We had a bit of time in Vancouver while we waited for our bus to Powell River. We had planned to go to Science World, but when we got there we found it was too expensive. So we went for a ride on the Sky Train and the Sea Bus to Lonsdale in West Vancouver, where we walked around, exploring the area.

There was a man we knew on the bus to Powell River. When we got there, he was kind enough to drive us home. When we got home, we lit the fires, had a cup of tea and went straight to bed.

A year later, in June 2000, we again decided to go to Princess Auto. This time, we were determined to go in the truck. The mechanics in our son Dan's shop had found the trouble with it overheating. It had been repaired and was ready to go. On June 14 we were off again. We left at 4:30 a.m., but a short way down the road, we went back to the house, as Charlie was not sure he had unplugged the electric kettle.

On our way again. Charlie was feeling strange, and we wondered if we were doing the right thing. This time, our truck was loaded with the 'cookie cutter' or, as we called it, 'the gizmo.' It was made of two bicycles—one right side up and the other upside down. A person would sit on the upright bike and pedal. The two bikes were joined by a chain which drove a bow saw and cut small wooden cookies off a small log. This is something that people of all ages everywhere have enjoyed. We have had it at fairs and schools.

The other inventions that we took were some of Charlie's all-terrain wheelchairs, his small steam engine and a couple of other small inventions.

It was raining hard, but it was not a hindrance to our travel, which was normal until we got to Hope, where traffic was slow due to an accident. There were also several delays due to construction. At one rest stop, going up the Fraser Canyon, we met a man who asked us which way to go to Vancouver. He had come down the Coquihalla from Kamloops and made a wrong turn at Hope. We told him he was going the wrong way, directed him back to Hope and the right road. Whether he ever got to Vancouver, we do not know.

At Cache Creek, we stopped for some gas. I went to the rest room, and on my way back to the truck the sun was in my eyes. I missed the step outside the building and fell flat on my face. I knocked my glasses off, bending the frame, hurt my knee and had a few other bruises. Charlie wondered if we should go on, but I told him "I hurt here and there, but I'm certainly able to travel." I had got my pants very dirty, as I had managed to fall into a puddle. I changed them that night when we stopped at a hotel in Kamloops. We had supper, a walk and a hot bath, and went off to bed.

Thursday:

Charlie was beginning to wonder if we should go on or not. After some discussion, we decided to continue. After several rest stops, meals and gas-ups, we found ourselves in Calgary, where we stayed for our second night out.

On Friday, we travelled as far as Maple Creek, Sask. On the way, in Brooks, Alberta, we needed our muffler fixed and the shifter had gone haywire. So we got that fixed as well as having the oil changed in the motor and transmission. The truck was in good condition again. However, on Saturday, we needed more repairs to the muffler. So, when we stopped at Morse, Saskatchewan we got that fixed.

We visited a very interesting museum in an old school building in Chaplin , Saskatchewan. The women there offered us tea and goodies after showing us through the museum and telling us some of their history. In Pelle Plain, Saskatchewan we took a walk around the town and seemed to be becoming more relaxed. Our motel was in Worsley, Saskatchewan that night.

Although I had thought we were doing OK when we got to Broadview, the next day, Charlie decided to go to the hospital for a checkup. He would not tell me why. The doctor there told him everything seemed fine. He told Charlie that he should relax more, but that he was fit to travel. We drove around the town a bit and headed out on the road again on our way to Manitoba.

As we had lots of time before the fair started, we drove around the town of Fleming and went for a walk, as well as visiting the Manitoba tourist Bureau. In Elkhorn, we went to the Auto Museum, where there are cars and trucks of all sizes, shapes, colors and ages.

There were no motels at Oak Lake Beach or Alexander. So it was late when we finally got one in Brandon. Before retiring, we went for a long walk around the area, which was very rural. We purchased some fish and chips and had them in our motel room, where we were able to make tea.

Tuesday, June 19, our 52nd anniversary:

After breakfast, we went out to the airfield, where we watched tha airplanes land and take off, viewed the hangars and went to the Airplane Museum, where we saw lots of old war planes.

In Austin, we went to their museum and got lots of good ideas for our Forest Museum here in Powell River. Charlie also went to the clinic for a blood test. Our hotel that night was in Portage La Prairie, where we had lots of time for a good walk before going to bed.

Oakville, Headlinger, and Winnipeg at last. It took a couple of wrong turns and backtracking before we found Princess Auto. We checked in with the staff, met some friends from the year before. Then we went to our hotel, where we watched TV and just relaxed, thankful that we had made it—now to get home again.

Wednesday was our day to relax. We went for a drive, took several walks, read, watched TV and took naps. We also had to get more muffler repairs done.

On Thursday, we went to the fair site and set up our display, after which we went for a walk and got my glasses frames adjusted. Back at the hotel, we just relaxed.

Friday was the first day of the inventor's fair. There were lots of people, from three-year olds to ninety-year olds, who tried the 'Gizmo' bicycle. People also tried out our all-terrain wheelchairs. One of the men from Princess Auto tried out a compressor on Charlie's little steam engine, which blew the pistons apart. So we fixed them and went back to the old tire pump. Kids of all ages liked to try working the steam engine using the tire pump. We have found the engine works well with a tire pump. We just connect the engine to the tire valve and let the air out. It runs the engine pretty fast.

Other inventions that I remember were a car ramp on the back of a pick-up and a system of crushing pop cans. There were many more, but I can't remember them. How I wish I had written them down in my notes, but then, I didn't know that I would be writing a book about them.

A man had a train of cars with seats big enough for one to sit in and he took people around the area outside. Of course, I had to have a ride.

One thing that happened in 1999 was our tour of the shops of Princess Auto. There, we saw how the different parts were made. It was very interesting to see how different pipes were formed. Some of the machinery was sure big. Princess Auto also has shops for maintenance and repair much the same as Canadian Tire. In fact, the store is very much like Canadian Tire.

Saturday, our second day at the show, was very much like the first, except that there was a banquet in the evening. It seemed a long way to go for a two-day show. We did not think we would do it again. It was the last show that we know of. We heard from another inventor that the following years of 2001 and 2002 were cancelled. During that last day, we packed up our gear so that we would be able to leave early the next morning for out trip home. At the banquet that night, Charlie told a joke about a policeman. You can imagine the laughter when it was discovered that the guest speaker was a policeman.

Sunday, June 21:

We were on our way home again. We started out at six in the morning. We had a hard time finding some place to eat that was open, until we got to Elm Creek, Manitoba, where we were able to get a cup of coffee at the station where we gassed up. There was a flea market at the junction of No. 2 and No. 10 Highways, where we were able to walk around, even though we did not buy anything. At Reston, Manitoba the garages and cafés were closed. I was desperate; so Charlie drove up a side road and I went in the bushes. After several more gas-ups, we were in Weyburn, Saskatchewan, where we discovered we had a flat tire. Luckily enough, there was a tire shop open nearby and we were able to get it fixed. As Charlie was not feeling well, we decided to get a motel and stay there that night. The A&W was our restaurant of choice in the evening. Monday, we headed out on the road again. Charlie seemed very frustrated and was afraid something was going to happen. I did not feel that way. I felt everything would be alright. In Assinobia, Charlie checked into the clinic again, where he was told everything was alright, but he should take things slower. We had lunch, then headed out on #2 Highway in Saskatchewan.

Just before Moose Jaw, we visited a very good museum. It was built like the old town, with wooden plank sidewalks and stores like they had been in the early part of the century. It was a wonderful place. Charlie got talking to some of the men there. So I walked around by myself, looking into all the buildings and other displays. They had a very good display of old farm machinery.

That night, we stayed in a motel in Herbert, Saskatchewan. We had decided, before we left the fair, that we would take a different route home from the one we took in coming. We took a route that had less traffic and found it was better for Charlie. He seemed less tense than before, but was still a bit tense, for some reason. We stopped more often, and I think that helped too.

We left the motel in Herbert at 5:30 in the morning. I'm not sure where it was, but I remember one motel that was isolated and shabby. There was a pub close by, and some wild-looking men came out of a very noisy place. We were glad to get out of there.

Another motel was more like a hotel. It was very plush—just the opposite of the previous one. It also had a nice park nearby where we could go for a walk. It was a real ritzy place. They served coffee and muffins in the morning. If I had known, at the time, that I would be writing about this trip, I would have taken better notes. As it is, this is mostly from memory. I only wrote things like the names of places we visited, with an occasional 'visited the museum,' but nothing about the museum or the area. I have vowed that I will do better, if we take any more trips like that.

Back to my story. Before lunch on Tuesday, June 27, we reached the border between Saskatchewan and Alberta. It was nice to feel that we were getting closer to home, even though I was enjoying myself. Charlie must have been anxious to get home, as he drove for miles without stopping. We only made stops to gas up, except for stops to read direction signs. We never even stopped to eat until we got to Fort McLeod, Alberta, where we had supper. Then we went on to Pinchard Creek, where we got a motel and fell into bed, very tired.

From Pinchard Creek, we went through the Crows Nest Pass without any problems. At Sparwood, we saw a huge mining tractor that was parked as a display outside a mall. We had lunch and phoned Krista to let her know that we would be at her home the next day. Outside of the town, we ran into road construction that was different from any we had seen before. There were about four or five machines working in a line. The first ripped up the old pavement, which went into the second machine to be ground up. The ground-up pavement was then laid back down where another machine rolled it out. Then, another machine seemed to pulverize the material and lay it down smoothly as pavement. It was amazing how those machines could take the old pavement up, process it and lay it down again as new pavement. It was all the same old material. It was unbelievable. We sat and watched those machines work for half an hour.

In Cranbrook, a lame man was having a hard time getting

around. Charlie helped him, as his wife could not. The couple insisted on buying us lunch. We then climbed a steep hill near Creston, where the truck temperature went up, but did not boil. We waited for it to cool down and went down the hill. We made a vehicle check at the bottom and found everything was OK. So we continued on into Rossland, where we got a motel for the night.

On Thursday, we left the motel at 6 a.m. to get an early start. It was better to drive in the early part of the day, when it was cooler. Also, there is not so much traffic. This was a more restful day—perhaps because we were getting closer to home. Charlie was relaxing more. We stopped at one place where there was a beautiful view of the mountains and valley. The Big Sheep Rest Area was a real wilderness picnic site, with tables in the bush. It was definitely not wheel-chair or handicapped accessible.

Near Christina Lake, we stopped at a rest area by a beautiful running creek. In Grand Forks, we found our favourite place, Robins, where we enjoyed coffee and donuts.

At last, Bridesville and Krista's. We settled in and went for a walk around the farm, happy to be there. Ralph, Krista's husband, had his parents visiting them at the time, so we only stayed overnight.

The next day, we stopped at Crawston to get some cherries, which were sure a treat.

Several more gas stops, a garage sale in Hedley, meal and rest stops and, surprisingly, we were on the 5:30 ferry from Horseshoe Bay. It was an hour late, so we had to rush to catch the 10:30 ferry from Earl's Cove.

June 30, 2000:

It had been a good trip, but frustrating at times. However, we were glad we had gone, but did not think we would do it again. If we had been younger, it would have been different. It we had gone slower and taken in the scenery, it would have been better.

Over the years, Charlie has invented many things. We had an old aeroplane prop that had been damaged. He cut the damaged tips off and came up with an air ice boat. We don't get ice on Cranberry lake often, but it would have been handy if we had had someone falling through the ice, as had happened a couple of times before. Fortunately, we never had to use it. One summer, we tried it out on a boat, and it became the airboat that we used to gather lily pads on the lake. The air prop was also used by some contractors as a fan to help with their trash burning.

Other inventions were two log transporters. One was a hand-operated lifter and the other fit behind our ATV. It was handy to get the dead and downed cedar out of the bush when we needed some material for our workshops at the schools and fairs. Charlie also invented a log lifter for his peavey, the Finland Candle and several other small inventions. He formed some garden hose into a circle and the kids would twirl it around their waists before the Hula Hoop came out. He also put the motor on the back of his loader before Hough Loaders came out. Just think, we could have been millionaires if he had patented some of his inventions. Oh well, we did fine the way it was, and have stayed happy.

In this book, I have written only about the longer trips that Charlie and I made. There were many shorter trips to see our daughters and our son, as well as trips in connection with our business, Basic Sawmill Training, and some pleasure trips.

Benita, our elder daughter, left home after her graduation from High School. She went to Kelowna, where she still lives with her family. We have made many trips to Kelowna to see her and our three grandchildren.

Krista married an RCMP officer who has been transferred several times. They have been in Vancouver, Kitimat and Dawson Creek, as well as a couple of other places. Since Ralph's retirement, they lived in Alberta before coming back to Bridesville in B.C. They manage a cattle ranch there. Charlie and I have made many trips to see Krista and our five grandchildren.

Marty, our youngest, moved first to Squamish and then to McKenzie to work in the logging industry. So there were trips to see him too. Then, of course, there were trips to see my grandmother in Kingston, Ontario and trips to see our friends from CUSO days. Of all of these trips, we have many memories.

Catalogue #04-1838

ISBN 1-41204031-0